S0-BAX-851

The
Salad-Green
Gardener

The
Salad-Green
Gardener

BARBARA CHIPMAN MOMENT

Illustrated by Julie Maas

Houghton Mifflin Company   Boston   1977

Copyright © 1977 by Barbara Chipman Moment

All rights reserved. No part of this work may be reproduced
or transmitted in any form by any means, electronic or
mechanical, including photocopying and recording, or by
any information storage or retrieval system, without
permission in writing from the publisher.

Library of Congress Cataloging in Publication Data
Moment, Barbara Chipman.
The salad green gardener.
Includes index.
1. Lettuce.   2. Salad greens.   3. Salads.
I. Title.
SB351.L6M65   635′ .5   76-46404
ISBN 0-395-25019-6
ISBN 0-395-25057-9 pbk.

Printed in the United States of America

A 10 9 8 7 6 5 4 3 2 1

For Jack

Contents

Introduction

A GARDENING BOOK just about lettuce and other salad greens? You bet! Look at lettuce. No other vegetable offers such a wide choice of varieties in taste, color, and texture. No other vegetable has so many growing possibilities. There are lettuces that don't go to seed or turn bitter in hot weather and some that are hardy enough to withstand light frosts. There are salad greens that you can grow all summer and some that you can leave in your garden all winter. Salad greens are beautiful in flower beds and borders. With a little care, you can grow them in pots on your porch and patio, in window boxes inside or outside of your apartment, and on your city terrace. You can even grow them in the cellar — lettuce and other salad greens are very accommodating. And they are good for you. Home-grown greens do not lose their nutritious value in the packing and shipping processes. They come to your salad bowl crisp, fresh and chock-full of vitamins and minerals that will pep you up but never fatten you up. They are not disease prone and they are not terribly fussy about the soil they grow in.

So, this is a book for gardeners to tell you all you need to know (and maybe more) in order to grow the best possible green salad ingredients, both outdoors and in. For ambitious salad buffs, there is a chapter on how to grow lettuce outdoors from nine to twelve months a year. Finally, there are recipes to help you enjoy the leafy greens of your labors.

The Salad-Green Gardener

Chapter One

A Short History of Lettuce

E VER SINCE lettuce was cultivated, some 2000 years ago, it has been lauded as a vegetable with exceptional powers. Kings, emperors, doctors, scholars, churchmen, herbalists, and folklore have all had something to say about the good and bad effects of eating and growing lettuce.

The Persian kings were eating lettuce as early as the sixth century B.C. Both the Greeks and the Romans cultivated a form of wild lettuce around the same period. Later, Hippocrates stated that he firmly believed lettuce "breeded the most laudable blood."

In the mythology of the Near East, the dead hero Tammuz (the Syrian and Babylonian equivalent of the Greek Adonis) was laid on a bed of lettuce for his annual descent into the subterranean world. Mourners carried urns of lettuce in his funeral procession to signify the close connection between animal and plant life — it was believed that both were short-lived and quickly faded.

At the beginning of the Christian era, the Romans prepared their lettuce by boiling it and then dousing it with oil and vinegar. This concoction, eaten after a meal, was supposed to be both a digestive aid and a sedative. Later, Romans ate their boiled lettuce before meals to whet their appetites for the more sensuous foods to come. Romans also considered lettuce to have the power to heal. The emperor Augustus, that "chief among equals," attributed his recovery from a high fever to lettuce. In gratitude for his return to robust health, he had an altar built and a statue erected to the "noble plant." The emperor Tacitus became very fond of lettuce and considered it a luxury in his otherwise frugal diet.

When the Romans conquered England, one of their friendlier acts was to introduce their diet of greens to their captives. Soon everyone in England was eating lettuce in the Roman manner. How long the English kept on boiling their lettuce is debatable. In the sixteenth century, John Gerard, the English herbalist, stated that "lettuce makes a pleasant salad, served raw with vinegar, oil and a little salt." At about the same time, Robert Burton, the English churchman and writer, wrote in his *Anatomy of Melancholy* that "salads are windy and not fit therefore to be eaten raw, though qualified with oyl, but in broths, or otherwise." There was a general agreement, however, that lettuce could cool the stomach, quench thirst, cause sleep, prevent hangovers, calm the nerves, provide abundant milk for nursing mothers, and restrain immoderate lust. Perversely, lettuce was also thought to have the power to arouse love. Nor is that the end of the astonishing powers of lettuce: English herbal folklore tells us that it is not a good idea to grow too much lettuce in the home garden as it could cause the wife to become sterile. Even eating a small amount of lettuce could adversely affect a wife's fertility.

In Europe, lettuce and most other salad greens disappeared during the Dark Ages and did not make a comeback until the Renaissance. The eighteenth and nineteenth centuries saw another salad scarcity which ended, finally, with the modern eating habits of the twentieth century.

In America, the first pilgrims, taking the tradition from their homeland, planted lettuce and other salad greens in their gardens, although in general, our Pilgrim Fathers considered "sallets" to be "women's food."

One of America's most devoted and passionate gardeners was Thomas Jefferson. In his *Garden Book* of 1774, he gave instructions for the planting of early vegetables including lettuce and many other greens. His salads of "mixed garden stuff" appeared regularly on the extravagant dinner menus at Monticello.

When Horace Greeley visited Denver in 1859, he found the miners' main diet to consist mainly of "bread, bacon and beans." But some improvements were on the way, since he also noted that there was a "man about the city yesterday with lettuce to sell . . ." Even so, Americans did not become avid salad eaters until the twentieth century.

The belief in the medicinal properties of lettuce has all but disappeared, although the juice of opium lettuce, a wild lettuce related to our cultivated varieties, is still used as an adulterant of opium in this country. All lettuces, in fact, wild and cultivated, contain a small amount of the same narcotic milky juice found in opium lettuce. No medicines are derived from it, although there are advocates of natural food remedies who prescribe eating lettuce regularly to calm the nerves and prevent insomnia.

Our garden lettuce is used to make soap, toilet water, and skin lotions. I have tried lettuce soap and I recommend it. I have also smoked several lettuce cigarettes. I do not recommend them.

Chapter Two

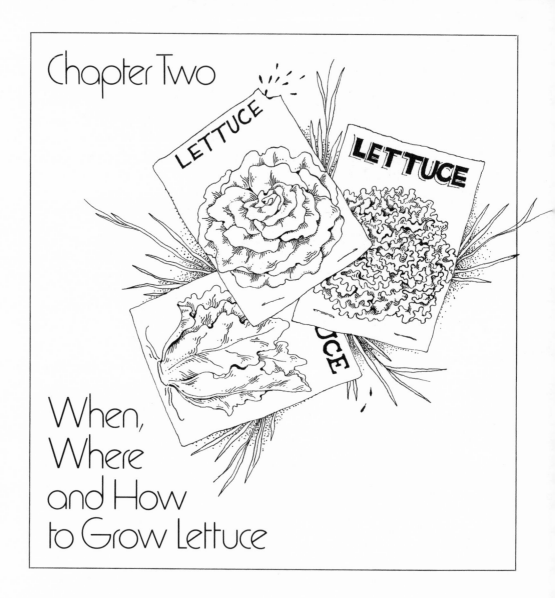

When, Where and How to Grow Lettuce

WHERE TO PLANT

"Plan your garden to suit yourself," a seasoned gardener once told me. I agree. But if you want to suit your *lettuce patch,* put it in a place that gets some shade during the day. I am fortunate in having a large ash tree that shades my plot for a few hours a day. If you don't have such an obliging tree, don't worry. You can easily make your own shade when your lettuce needs it during the hot summer days, and I'll tell you how later on in this chapter. Put your lettuce patch where it is most convenient, but not in a hollow where water could collect and rot your seeds and plants.

Lettuce can be grown next to any other vegetables. Interplanting it with chives, onions, radishes, garlic, and herbs helps repel bugs. Carrots planted next to lettuce will give it some protection from the summer sun. If you have the room, plant a little kitchen garden near your back door and grow your lettuce and other greens along with the herbs you use in salads and cooking. If you want to be fancy and somewhat extravagant, you can make a raised bed with redwood boards nailed to posts. This makes a neat and handsome salad garden.

The size of your lettuce patch depends, of course, on your particular needs. I grow my lettuce in a 6 by 10-foot area, which is large enough to keep a family of four salad-lovers happy, with extra lettuce to give away. If you are short on space, you can tuck lettuce between rows of slower-ripening vegetables and in other spots in your vegetable and flower gardens.

SOIL FOR LETTUCE

Some gardeners say that lettuce will thrive in any well-drained soil. I won't argue with this statement, but I will add to it because I like to give lettuce every opportunity to grow as large and healthy as it possibly can. Soil for lettuce should be dug deep, 1 to 2 feet, and kept loose and moist. If your soil is hard and claylike, dig some sand and humus (rotted compost) or peat moss into it. I give my soil a dose of nutrients before I plant because lettuce is a fast grower and needs its food in the ground to begin with. Vegetable meals such as cottonseed, soybean, and peanut will give your soil the nitrogen, phosphorus, and potash that lettuce thrives on. Blood meal, bone meal, seaweed-derived materials, and fish emulsions are also good. Follow the directions on the package for the amounts to use and don't worry if you happen to give your soil an overdose — one of the advantages of using organic fertilizers is that they break up slowly in the soil and won't burn your plants. If you use raw manure be sure to dig it well into the ground. Midseason, I give my soil a boost with blood meal, but you can use whatever organic fertilizer you have on hand — your lettuce plants will grow with renewed vigor and your seedlings will be off to a good start.

Lettuce does best in a slightly alkaline soil. You can find out if your soil is acid or alkaline (your soil's pH) by sending a sample of it to your local agricultural agent or you can test it with a simple home testing kit available at most garden centers. A pH of 7 is neutral. Any number below 7 is acid; any number above is alkaline.

If your soil tests from $6\frac{1}{2}$ to $7\frac{1}{2}$ on the pH scale, you are within the normal limits for growing lettuce and most other salad greens. If you find that your soil is very acid, add crushed limestone, dolomite, or wood ashes to it. (Five pounds of crushed limestone is enough for 100 square feet, and will last for about three years.) If your soil is very alkaline, add peat moss, cottonseed meal, pine needles, or oak leaves.

I can't leave this discussion without telling you about some fun I had planting lettuce in Maine last summer. Down by the lake there are two rotting logs side by side with a mixture of moss, pine needles, and rotted leaves between them. It is a nice cool spot that gets the afternoon sun. Being a bit of a lettuce maniac, I thought it would be interesting to see if I could grow lettuce in the spongy and very acid soil between the logs. I had a packet of leaf lettuce with me and I sowed a row of seeds between the logs and gave them a good drink of lake water. Four days later, there was a row of spunky green seedlings just as strong as if they had been started in my best garden soil. At the end of the summer, I transplanted them into a small flat, brought them home with me, and transplanted them again into my garden. I harvested my "log lettuce" until the first killing frost.

Now I didn't tell you this story so that you will ignore all the good advice I've given you on soil for lettuce — I only wanted to give the "any well-drained soil" fellows a fair shake.

WHEN TO PLANT

Lettuce is a hardy vegetable and is one of the first you can plant: in early spring, 4 to 6 weeks before the last frost, or as soon as the ground is workable, as the seed packets tell you. If you have a mulch on your garden, either left on year round or put on the previous fall, the ground will be workable as soon as you pull the mulch back. If your garden is not mulched, your soil will be workable when a handful of it falls apart when you squeeze it. Rake the soil smooth and sow your seeds.

In New York State, where I live, I plant looseleaf and butterhead lettuce varieties around the middle to end of March (weather permitting) in the garden. As crisphead lettuce takes from 60 to 80 days to mature and does not head well in hot weather, I start it indoors about 4 to 6 weeks *before* the ground is workable and transplant it into the garden at the time I sow the looseleaf and butterhead varieties. Before transplanting young plants into the garden, they must be "hardened off" for about 2 weeks. This means getting them used to the outdoor weather. A coldframe is an ideal place to harden off plants, but if you don't have a coldframe, you can put your plants outdoors for a few hours a day. During the hardening-off period, cut down the amount of water you give the plants by half. On the day you transplant them, water them well with a liquid fertilizer such as seaweed or fish emulsion to give them a good start.

If you don't want to start crisphead lettuce indoors, you can plant it directly in the coldframe 4 to 6 weeks before transplanting it into the garden. Butterhead lettuce may also be started indoors or in a coldframe. You can do the same with looseleaf lettuce, but I don't think it is worth the trouble as it matures so rapidly.

Lettuce can, and should, be planted in midsummer for a fall crop — a subject I go into quite thoroughly later on in this chapter. In areas where springs are long and cool, crisphead lettuce can be sown directly into the garden along with looseleaf and butterhead varieties.

HOW TO PLANT

I used to plant lettuce exactly as I was told to on the seed packets. I don't anymore. I never did like getting out strings and stakes to make straight rows and I was always afraid I wasn't putting enough dirt on top of the seeds or else I was burying them forever. What I do now is plant my lettuce in groups, sowing 4 to 6 seeds in each group and allowing 6 inches of space around each group. This group planting method is a real space saver — you can grow a large crop of lettuce in a space approximately 3 by 3 feet. Instead of making furrows, I put the seeds where I want them and simply step on them and do not put any dirt on top of them at all. I learned this trick from a Maine gardener.

Once you plant the seeds or, rather, step on them, moisten the ground using a hose with a fine spray; keep the ground moist to assure germination. When the plants are 3 inches high or have 4 leaves, thin them out, leaving the strongest plant in each group. Make sure your head lettuce plants have 10 to 12 inches between them.

Of course lettuce will grow perfectly well when planted in rows, but I think the group planting method is a lot easier and you waste far less seed. You don't have to waste the seedlings you thin out, either, You can eat them or you can transplant them into another part of your patch or garden.

HOW TO TRANSPLANT

It's easy to transplant lettuce — just don't do it on a hot, sunny day. Hold the seedling by the leaves and dig it up, keeping a clump of dirt on its roots. (I use an old teaspoon.) Make a hole in the soil and plant the seedling just deep enough so that the first leaves rest on the surface of the soil. Press the soil around the seedling, making sure there are no depressions left in the soil that could hold water and cause the seedling to rot. Water the seedling and pull some mulch around it.

You can retard the growth of a seedling by shaking off all the soil from its roots. This removes the tiny feeder roots from the main ones and will set back the growth of the seedling by about two weeks. This is a good method of controlling the growth rate of your plants to stagger the number of mature plants in your lettuce patch. But be sure to plant the seedling quickly so the roots do not dry out.

SUCCESSIVE PLANTINGS

The seed packets tell you to make successive plantings every two weeks until the middle of June and then wait until midsummer to plant for a fall crop. But what about the lettuceless time in between? Back to the market? Certainly not. You can avoid this costly and unnecessary salad gap by growing what I call "standby lettuce." Here's how:

Two or three weeks after you have made your initial planting in the garden, seed one or two flats (use pots if you don't have flats) with several varieties of lettuce; label them. Keep the flats next to the garden for convenience's sake and be careful not to let the soil dry out; it does so more quickly than in the garden. When the seedlings are 3 inches high, or have 4 leaves, thin them out to 2 inches apart, leaving the strongest plants for transplanting. When you have a space in your lettuce patch or in any other part of your garden, simply transplant the seedlings from the flats to the garden. What you are doing is making successive plantings with plants instead of seeds.

When I use up the seedlings in my flats, I reseed them, sowing warm-weather varieties around the first of June and cool-weather varieties in midsummer. I think "standby lettuce" is worth the small amount of effort it takes. It lets you have lettuce plants in your garden all of the time, *maturing at different rates,* and it saves space. If there is an extreme hot spell, you can move your flats into the shade. And you will always have plants handy in case of disasters — cats and dogs digging in your garden, a washout rain, your best friend's toddler stepping on your seedlings, and anything else that could cause havoc in your lettuce patch. "Standby lettuce" is dependable.

SURPRISE LETTUCE

Another way to get "standby lettuce" is to broadcast a mixture of new or leftover lettuce seeds (and other salad green seeds) in your garden in the spring in a section where you plan to plant warm-weather vegetables later on. Not only does this method of planting give you seedlings for transplanting into your lettuce patch, it gives you a surprise mixture of young greens for your salad bowl. I say "surprise" because when I have done this I never remember what varieties I've sown.

SHADE FOR LETTUCE

By July, your lettuce will need some shade to keep it from bolting: growing a thick flower stalk, turning bitter, and going to seed. Even the heat-resistant varieties appreciate some protection from the summer sun. One way to make shade quickly and easily is to use thin, 3-foot bamboo poles and cheesecloth. Push the poles into the ground around your lettuce patch and down the middle, keeping the poles about 3 feet apart. Then drape a single layer of cheesecloth over them and secure it to the poles with Twistoms. Leave the north side of the tent open so you can get at your lettuce. Finish off the job by putting rocks around the bottom of the cheesecloth to keep it from blowing away.

For a super-cooling effect in hot weather, sprinkle the cheesecloth with a hose, using a fine spray. You will be surprised how effective this is. Your lettuce will stay sweet and tender during even the worst dog days.

An alternative to making your own shade for your lettuce is to grow it in the shade of other vegetables — between the cabbage rows, in the harvested asparagus patch, or between rows of corn.

PLANTING A FALL CROP

It's August and your summer lettuce is doing fine and you are determined you will have your own garden lettuce up until the first killing frost. Good for you! But be sure to choose varieties that take no longer to mature than the time left before the first hard frost in your area. You wouldn't want to plant a variety of lettuce on August 15 that takes 70 to 80 days to mature if you get killing frosts by September 15. (See the map on page 141 to find the average date of the first fall frost in your area.) Be sure that the soil is moist when you plant.

Whether you plant seeds directly in the ground or in flats for your fall lettuce crop, your seeds will not germinate quickly in the hot weather. There are ways you can easily overcome this problem.

FREEZING SEEDS

The simplest way to assure fast germination is to put your seeds in a paper cup, plastic bag, or aluminum foil and set them in your freezer for a day before you sow them. Another method, which I haven't tried myself, is to freeze your seeds in an ice tray full of tea and then plant each cube. My neighbor, who told me about this, swears by it.

SPROUTING SEEDS

A little more trouble, but absolutely foolproof, is sprouting your seeds first. To do this, either soak your seeds in half a cup of water for two days, or sprinkle them on a wet paper towel, enclose them in a plastic bag, tie it shut, and leave it in a dim place for two days. Either way, the seeds will swell and grow a tiny sprout, which you must handle gently or it will break off. When you plant sprouted seeds, lay them flat and cover them with a very little soil (don't step on them this time) and keep them moist. Last summer I planted some unsprouted seeds next to some sprouted ones and found that the unsprouted seeds took five days to come up while the sprouted ones appeared in two.

CELLAR LETTUCE

It was a hot day in August, a real scorcher. I couldn't find our new puppy anywhere. Finally, after calling and whistling and looking behind and under the furniture, I went down to the cellar. There he was in a corner of the laundry room under a table. He was all wags and wiggles, glad to see me, but not in the least willing to leave his cool spot. Smart puppy, I thought, it's like a spring day down here. Of course! Perfect lettuce weather. Half an hour later, I had seeded a flat with two fast-maturing varieties of looseleaf lettuce and a new frost-resistant crisphead, called Evergreen.

12

Four days later, the seedlings were up and now needed more light. The cellar door was open, the sun was shining in, but it was still cool on the cellar steps. I put my flat on the bottom step where it was the coolest but still got five hours of afternoon sun. When the plants were 3 inches high, I transplanted them into my lettuce patch, watered and mulched them. They provided me with a fine crop of early and late fall lettuce, as sweet and tasty as any lettuce I've grown in the spring. A cool cellar, I've also found, is an excellent place to grow lettuce and other salad greens any time of the year under lights.

HARVESTING LETTUCE

The best time to pick lettuce and salad greens is when the sun is at its highest because the vitamin C content will be at its peak then. With all leafy vegetables, the stronger the light, the higher the amount of vitamin C. Leafy vegetables lose vitamin C when they are stored for long, so best pick your lettuce and other greens on the day you are going to use them.

When I thin my lettuce I am also harvesting it, as I use the thinnings in my salads. The little plants are sweet and tender and I sometimes fill an entire salad bowl with them. When I harvest mature looseleaf lettuce, I pick the outer leaves as I need them and the plants keep growing new leaves. With butterhead and crisphead varieties, I pull up the entire plant. However, heading lettuce can be cut off a little above ground level and the stump will keep producing new leaves. This is a good thing to do in the fall when it is too late to plant head lettuce.

Please don't let your lettuce sit in the ground and grow old — it will become tough and bitter if you do. Better to give it away while it's young if you can't use it, or add it to your compost heap.

After you pick your lettuce, wash it in a deep pan of cold water, dry it well, put it in a plastic bag, and store it in the refrigerator. Getting garden lettuce dry is important if you want it to get nice and crisp for you. Last year, a friend told me about a salad spinner. It is a terrific gadget and every lettuce grower should have one. There are several versions of salad spinners on the market, but they all work on the same principle, which is to get rid of the water clinging to the lettuce leaves by centrifugal action. I use my salad spinner for all my green salad vegetables. You can also dry your lettuce in a string bag and swing it around your head — but you have to go outdoors to do that.

COLLECTING AND SAVING SEEDS

The price of vegetable seeds this year is twenty per cent higher than last year. This is due, I read, to the large demand from the increasing number of home gardeners. Even if the price continues to rise I'm not sure you'll save much money by harvesting your own seeds, but you might enjoy doing it. Whatever you do, don't throw away packaged seeds, as they last from five to seven years. Store them with your other vegetable seeds in envelopes in a box (not airtight) in a dry place at room temperature. Don't forget to label the envelopes with the names of the seeds and the year they were purchased.

To save lettuce seeds from your garden, choose healthy plants, put a stake near each one, and label it. As lettuce is pretty well self-pollinating, you don't have to worry that any of the varieties you choose will be cross-pollinated. When the plants have developed a tall stalk and have flowered, tie them to the stakes to keep them from falling over. Let the seeds ripen in the garden for a week, then pull up the entire plant and hang it upside down to dry in a warm, airy place. To clean the seeds, which you can do in the winter or spring, pick them out of the pods or use a wire screening with a small mesh to sift out the chaff. Label and store the seeds as you would your packaged seeds.

Before you use your seeds, find out whether or not they are fertile by scattering a dozen on a sponge or paper towel in a shallow dish and adding enough water to the dish to keep the seeds moist. Keep the dish in a warm, dark place and note what percentage of them sprout and how long they take to do so. If the seeds get moldy and do not send out any sprouts, don't use any from the plant you took the test seeds from. If you allow the seeds to dry out, you'll have to start the test all over again. Sorry.

MULCHING

Lettuce and other salad greens thrive in a cool, moist soil. Bare soil is likely to dry up, causing the plants to wilt, their leaves to shrivel and lose their vitamins. Mulching also means less work because it keeps the soil moist and friable and the weeds down. There are many suitable mulch materials that you don't have to buy, such as leaves, grass clippings, pine needles, sawdust, shredded newspapers, and even stones.

If you want to make the most beautiful mulch imaginable, buy yourself a "shredder." You can put all your dead leaves, flower and vegetable plants, hedge clippings, even the branches of your Christmas tree into the hopper of this magical machine. Out will come, into a bag, what I call "garden confetti" — tiny pieces of mulch from your backyard wastes. You can also buy salt hay, peat moss, wood or bark chips, and black plastic. When mulching, you should add a little extra fertilizer to the soil, as all organic mulches take nitrogen from the soil when they decompose. Don't apply any mulch until your lettuce and other salad greens are well up and have been thinned. Then water the soil and put down a 3-inch mulch. As the weather grows hotter and the weeds become more persistent, make the mulch thicker. If you see weeds coming up through the mulch, smother them with more mulch. With this treatment your salad plants and all your other vegetables will be a lot healthier. A mulched garden allows you freedom. You don't have to rush out to water at the first sign of a dry spell; you can even go away for a two-week vacation without asking your neighbor to water your garden for you. Mulching also protects your lettuce and other salad greens in cold weather. I have gotten through several frosts without losing my lettuce crop because it was protected with mulch.

YEAR-ROUND MULCHING

This is the famous method developed by Ruth Stout, the veteran no-work gardener. Her method eliminates all need for hoeing, cultivating, raking, weeding, compost making, rotating crops, and adjusting the soil's pH. Your garden becomes your compost heap. You feed your soil all year by putting garden wastes and all kitchen garbage except meat scraps under the blanket of permanent mulch.

It doesn't matter when you start building up your permanent mulch, the important thing is to begin. When it is time to plant in the spring, you pull back the mulch and sow your seeds, then wait until the plants are well up and have been thinned before you put the mulch back around the plants.

I have used Ruth Stout's method with great success. My vegetables flourish and my soil is rich and black and crumbly. There are so many earthworms working the soil under the mulch I sometimes think I've started an earthworm farm.

INTENSIVE GARDENING

Maybe you don't like the idea of putting your garbage in your vegetable garden and leaving it permanently mulched. Or you simply don't agree with that method. Some gardeners believe the Ruth Stout way of gardening is too messy and that it is too difficult to push the mulch aside or poke down through it to sow seeds. They also believe it is misleading to tell anyone you can have a garden with little or no work by keeping it heavily mulched; a good garden is the result of well-thought-out planning and hard work. They advise spreading a heavy mulch on your garden in the fall, taking it off in the spring, and saving your garbage for the compost pile.

In general, the rule for intensive gardening is to plant closer together and to cultivate the soil until the plants are large enough to touch one another. Specifically, for lettuce, this is how you do it: Plant your lettuce sparingly in groups or in rows 12 inches apart and make successive plantings every two weeks until June and then again in August. As soon as the plants are several inches high, cultivate them, using a narrow rake or potato hook. Be careful not to cultivate too deeply, as the roots of lettuce are shallow. This early cultivating gets a jump on the weeds and stirs up the soil to keep it healthy. It is always best to cultivate after a rain, but not while the ground is soggy. As soon as the weeds begin to show, cultivate again.

Thin leaf lettuce when it is 2 inches high to stand 4 to 5 inches apart in the rows. Thin head lettuce when it is also 2 inches high, leaving one plant every 8 to 10 inches in the rows. (Treat endive the same as head lettuce.) Keep cultivating. By the middle of July there will be little weeding to do as the tops of the mature plants will touch each other, causing a greenhouse effect on the soil which will keep it moist and weed-free. Gardeners who use this method say you can get more plants per foot in your garden than you can from one that is cluttered up with mulch, and that mulching between the rows takes just as much time as cultivating.

BROADCAST PLANTING

Another method of intensive gardening is to broadcast, or scatter, seed over a smoothly raked seed bed. Plants come up thickly, using up every inch of ground and, because they are so crowded, they never grow into mature plants. Looseleaf lettuce and other leafy greens are especially suited for this method, as they are at their best when harvested while young and tender. Crowding also causes the plants to be of different shapes and sizes. As you harvest and make space, the smaller plants will have room to grow and produce a second crop.

A lot of fertilizer is needed for this type of intensive planting, as the nutrients in the soil are used up quickly.

If you have limited space this intensive gardening plan is a good one to try.

MAKING A COMPOST PILE

I think a compost pile is a good thing to have no matter how you garden. You can use compost in your flower garden, when you transplant seedlings, to enrich the soil for container gardening, and in new gardens. You can begin making a compost pile any time of the year, but fall is best because the growing season is over and there is a plentiful supply of waste materials.

Because compost is decayed organic matter, the smaller the pieces of waste that go into the pile, the faster they will break down and the finer your compost will be. Here is where a shredder machine is a great help. You can also use your power mower to run over material, particularly leaves, which mat heavily.

The size of the pile you make is up to you. A 2 by 4-foot area built up to a height of 3 feet is a good size for the average backyard garden. I prefer several small piles as opposed to one large one.

There are many ways to make a compost pile, but here is one of the easiest and quickest ways I know of. It is also odorless. Pick a sunny place near your vegetable garden so you don't have to go far to transfer the compost. Start by loosening the soil with a rake or hoe in the compost area to expose the bacteria in the soil — those good little animals which are going to work so hard for you. Then make layers of the materials you have handy, alternating kitchen wastes with garden waste materials, such as grass clippings, leaves, sod, and weeds. Unless your soil is very alkaline, put some wood ashes on the layers, too, and while you are at it, sprinkle on some blood meal or other organic fertilizer containing a high percentage of nitrogen to speed decomposition. Water the pile well and cover it with black plastic and weight the plastic down with stones, bricks, or dirt. Every time you get an accumulation of kitchen and garden wastes — save them in a garbage pail or large plastic bag — add them to the pile in alternating layers. Be sure to cover the pile each time with the plastic. Under plastic, the temperature of the pile should reach approximately 140° F. on a sunny day. You can add more nitrogen to the middle of the pile if you see that it is not decomposing, but this is usually unnecessary.

You can use your compost in your vegetable garden when it is still crumbly and not completely decayed. A small handful of this compost put into the hole when you are transplanting lettuce will give the young seedling a real boost.

For a finer soil to use in flower pots and window boxes, let the compost "cook" longer.

GREENHOUSE LETTUCE

If you have a greenhouse you can grow superb looseleaf and butterhead lettuce all winter long. Lettuce and other salad greens are excellent crops for greenhouses because they grow fast and produce large yields in a relatively small space. Their basic needs are good distribution of moisture through the soil, a humid atmosphere, and cool temperatures: 50°–55° F. at night and 60°–70° F. by day. Use one of the soil mixes I describe on page 80 and sow the seeds thinly on top of the soil. Press the seeds into the soil, water with a fine spray, and cover with a newspaper until the seeds germinate. When the seedlings are up, uncover them. Thin the seedlings to 8 to 10 inches apart. Be sure to keep the plants well watered and to fertilize them every two weeks.

The best time to make your first planting is at the end of August. Then make successive plantings every three weeks until it is time to plant your lettuce and other salad greens in the garden again — in other words, spring.

Chapter Three

A Lettuce Seminar

A N ENTHUSIASTIC GARDENER, writing in the early 1920's, said that he was forever amazed at the limited variety of lettuce available in the market when the home grower could choose from over twenty varieties listed in one seed catalog. Having been allured since boyhood by the magic of the seed catalogs, he was thankful there were so many lettuces to choose from, even if some of them added no basic improvement over the older kinds. He found, as I have, that there is charm in novelty itself, and in the true spirit of the home gardener, he learned that experimenting with the different varieties was half the fun of growing his own fresh lettuce — lettuce he could eat, as he said, "before the life had begun to go out of it."

I don't know how many varieties of lettuce there are available for home growers today. I do know that many of the same ones appear under different names in the various catalogs. To sort them all out and match them up would take more time than I'd care to part with, as would growing them all to discover the pros and cons of each of the improvements and subtle variations. It makes my head spin to think of it. And yet, when the seed catalogs arrive, I can't wait to search out the latest prizewinners in the lettuce world. Last year I grew Slobolt lettuce for the first time and was so pleased with the way it lived up to its name that it is now on my permanent lettuce list.

It would be needless for me (and boring to you) to name all the varieties of lettuce in the many catalogs listed at the back of this book. My purpose is to tell you about my favorites and those that have been recommended to me by my gardening friends. It is possible that some I have had success with, you may find to be dismal failures. This we can blame on the variations in overall growing conditions in the different sections of the country, the whims of weather, and your own determination for success. So do consult the catalogs — they give you excellent advice about the best lettuces to grow in your particular area.

To simplify matters, I have divided the varieties of lettuce into two main categories: head and looseleaf. Cos, or romaine, lettuce is sometimes given its own category as it grows into an upright stalk, but as it is also a crisphead type, into that category it goes.

The varieties of lettuce in each of the following lists are ordered by their

Crisphead

heat-resistant qualities, going, in general, from those which can stand the most heat to those which can stand the coldest temperatures.

HEAD LETTUCE

There are two kinds of head lettuce: crisphead and butterhead. Crisphead has a firm, tightly folded head, a brittle texture, and a mild, sweet taste. Butterhead forms a smaller, loosely folded head and has a soft texture with a sweet, buttery taste.

CRISPHEAD

Name	Days to Maturity	Features
Ithaca	72	Dark green, frilled leaves. Resistant to tipburn. An excellent iceberg-type lettuce.
Imperial No. 44	84	Dark green, heavily savoyed leaves. Medium-large heads.

Hot Weather	82	Frilled leaves surround blanched heads. Doesn't go bitter in hot weather.
Great Lakes	90	Large, dark green, thick leaves. Forms heads even in hot weather.
Ballerina	80	Small, compact heads. Resistant to tipburn.
Parris Island Romaine	76	Forms firm heads 10 inches high. Hearts blanch nearly white. More piquant taste than other crispheads. Resistant to mildew and mosaic.
Valmaine Romaine	75	Similar to Parris Island. Resistant to mildew and mosaic.
Midget Romaine	70	Grows only 5 inches tall. Tender, sweet hearts. A superior romaine; slow to bolt.

Romaine

Paris White Romaine	83	Light green leaves, self-blanching, endivelike flavor. A favorite in northern states.
New York Special	65	A new variety developed for gardeners in the eastern U.S. Cabbagelike 10-inch heads. Does best in spring and fall.
Premier Great Lakes	93	Resistant to tipburn. An early spring lettuce.
Pennlake	85	Solid, conical heads. Leaves less ribby than Great Lakes. Does best in cool weather. Resistant to tipburn.
Evergreen	95	Dark green leaves. Grows taller than other crispheads. Excellent for a fall crop.
Arctic King	80	Light green, crinkly leaves. Very hardy. Sow in fall to winter over for early spring crop.

BUTTERHEAD

| Fordhook | 78 | Glossy, dark green outer leaves, creamy yellow hearts. A real winner. |
| Butter King | 70 | Largest of the butterheads. Medium green leaves. Disease resistant. |

Buttercrunch	65	A Bibb lettuce. Small, loose head. Doesn't go bitter in heat. A favorite.
Summer Bibb	70	Compact round heads, small dark green leaves. Medium heat resistant.
Tom Thumb	65	Looks like a small Bibb lettuce. Delicate, delicious, superb.
Deer Tongue or Matchless	80	A small lettuce with dark green leaves. Grows upright, tastes somewhat bland. Does best in cool weather but can also stand heat.
Dark Green Boston	80	Dark green, thick leaves. Mosaic resistant. A cool-weather lettuce.
Big Boston	75	Broad, smooth leaves. A cool-weather lettuce.

LOOSELEAF LETTUCE

Looseleaf, or nonheading, lettuce has the well-founded reputation of being the easiest lettuce to grow and is the most popular for home growers. It is a pretty lettuce, too. I like to look at the pictures of looseleaf lettuce on the seed packets — there are dark and light green leaves, red-tipped and reddish-bronze leaves, frilled, wavy, crumpled, and deeply lobed leaves. And, as if it weren't just enough to look at it, looseleaf lettuce is said to be higher in food value than the blanched varieties. I have only one complaint about looseleaf lettuce — it is a bit too mild tasting for my liking. To remedy this, I combine looseleaf lettuce with other kinds of lettuce and salad greens in my tossed salads.

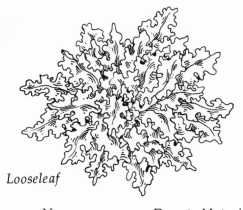

Looseleaf

Butterhead

Name	Days to Maturity	Features
Slobolt	45	Light green, frilled leaves with thick clusters at the center. Lasts all summer.
Oakleaf	45	Oak-shaped leaves form a loose head. Very slow to bolt and also very hardy. Can be wintered over.
Salad Bowl	45	Bright green leaves spread like a flower over 1½ feet. Slow to bolt and resists light frosts. An old favorite.
Green Ice	45	Crisp, dark green, savoyed leaves. Slow to bolt.
Ruby	45	Bright green leaves tipped with red. Best eaten when young. Insect resistant. A pretty lettuce.

Prizehead	45	Curled green leaves are shaded a brownish red.
Black-Seeded Simpson	45	Light, lime green leaves, some crinkled. Blanched center leaves. A cool-weather lettuce which is an old favorite.
Grand Rapids	45	Light green, frilled leaves. Tipburn resistant. A cool-weather lettuce.
Domineer	40	Similar to Grand Rapids but has darker leaves. Very hardy. Can be wintered over.

SEED TAPES AND PELLETED SEEDS

Some of the varieties of lettuce in the above lists are available in seed tapes and pelleted seeds. (Check your catalogs for the varieties available.) Seed tapes were invented to save you the trouble of spacing seeds and to eliminate the need for extra thinning. They are more expensive than regular seeds. I have never tried them and I do not really see the advantages with leafy vegetables, where thinnings are so useful. Pelleted seeds are seeds that are coated to make them easier to sow and again to eliminate extra thinning. They are also more expensive than regular seeds. I have never tried these either.

Chapter Four

Enemies of Lettuce

ESPITE THE ominous title of this chapter and the following list of diseases and pests, I have found that lettuce has few problems — certainly not worth losing a night's sleep over. If your soil is healthy, that is, rich in humus and minerals, you can grow robust lettuce that resists disease and bugs. Just in case your lettuce does meet up with an "enemy" or two, here are the most common.

DISEASES

TIPBURN

Tipburn is the most common of lettuce problems. The name of the disease describes what it is: the tips of the leaves turn yellow, then brown, and the leaf dies. Tipburn is caused by the lettuce plants losing water during hot, dry weather.

REMEDIES

Keep the ground moist and mulch the plants.

Plant lettuce varieties that withstand the disease: Premier Great Lakes, Grand Rapids, Pennlake, Ithaca, Ballerina.

Don't fertilize plants in warm weather.

MOSAIC OR YELLOW LEAVES

Mosaic deforms and mottles lettuce leaves. As the disease advances, the leaves turn yellow and the plants become stunted and eventually die. Mosaic is a virus disease spread by aphids and leafhoppers and sometimes by ants.

REMEDIES

Plant lettuce varieties that are tolerant of mosaic: Parris Island Romaine, Valmaine Romaine, Dark Green Boston.

Remove affected plants and throw them in the garbage.

Remove weeds around the lettuce patch, especially wild aster, wild carrot, dandelion, and wild chicory.

To avoid spreading the virus, don't smoke in your garden (if you do smoke, is wet.

Destroy aphids and leafhopper nests (see Insects below).

Mildew

Mildew is a fatal disease caused by a fungus. Mildew produces light yellow and light green spots on mature lettuce leaves, then the leaves turn white and moldy and the plant dies.

REMEDIES
Plant resistant varieties: Parris Island Romaine, Valmaine Romaine.
Destroy the diseased plants.

Bottom Rot

Bottom rot causes the bottom leaves of lettuce plants to turn reddish brown and slimy. It is a disease caused by long spells of wet weather and will disappear when the weather dries up.

REMEDIES
Plant upright romaine varieties.
Be sure the soil is well drained.

INSECTS

Aphids

Aphids are tiny insects of many colors and shapes. The mosaic-spreading aphids are yellowish green. Aphids are found on the undersides of leaves, where they suck the juices out of the leaves, causing them to curl.

REMEDIES
The best remedy is to be sure your soil is healthy, free of weeds, and well mulched.

Pick leaves affected by aphids and destroy them.

Wash aphids off leaves with a hose.

Spray plants with soap and water.

Spray plants once a week with a mixture of 1 part water and 1 part milk.

Buy ladybugs and praying mantises — they love to eat aphids.

Plant garlic, chives, onions, French marigolds, and other flowers with strong scents around your garden.

LEAFHOPPERS

Leafhoppers are tiny wedge-shaped insects, usually green in color. They can jump incredible distances and are also good flyers. Like aphids, they suck the juices out of plants from the undersides of leaves, causing the leaves to curl and their tips to turn brown.

Destroy the leafhoppers' nests before the adults emerge. You can easily recognize their nests — they are globs of spittlelike foam which appear in spring on plant stalks.

Attract birds that eat leafhoppers: flycatchers, phoebes, warblers, and gnat-catchers are attracted by marigolds, California poppies, and sunflowers.

Cutworms

These soft little worms are usually found right beneath the surface of the soil. When you disturb them they curl up tightly. They come in colors of gray, white, light brown, black, and gray-green. Their damage to young plants is devastating, as they spend their nights chewing off plants at their base. They hide under the soil during the day.

REMEDIES

The simplest and best control is to put a cardboard or paper collar around the young plants. Make a collar 3 inches high and 1½ inches in diameter. Set the collar 1 inch deep into the ground. You can also use a milk carton cut off at both ends.

Keep your garden free of weeds so the cutworm moth will not have a place to lay its eggs.

Get a toad.

Interplant your lettuce and other plants with onions.

Cabbage Worms

These are pale green worms that eat large holes in lettuce and cabbage leaves.

REMEDIES

Pick worms off leaves.

Sprinkle wood ashes around plants.

Sprinkle with salt water every morning until pests disappear.

Spray plants with Bacillus Thuringiensis, a biological control spray.

Release trichogramma wasps — parasites which are nearly invisible and harmless to plants and people.

WHITEFLIES

These terrible pests have been nicknamed "garden dandruff" and for good reason. When disturbed from sucking the juices out of leaves, they fly in the air in a cloud of white specks. They have the unfortunate ability to multiply rapidly and are, as a result, hard to control.

REMEDIES

The trichogramma wasp is being used effectively against whiteflies.

Spray the unhatched whiteflies on the undersides of the leaves with a spray made up of 1 quart water, ½ teaspoon Tabasco, 1 teaspoon garlic powder, and a dash of liquid detergent. Shake well or mix in a blender. Or try a spray made up of 1 part molasses and 50 parts water.

SLUGS

I won't carry on about how much I dislike this slimy pest or the hours I've spent trying to defeat it, but I will tell you that I consider the slug to be lettuce's cleverest and most enduring enemy.

Although, for convenience, I list it under Insects, a slug is actually a mollusk without a shell. It never gets enough to eat, but it works at trying to every night of its life and in early mornings too. It cannot stand hot sun so it hides under anything that will provide a cool, dark place during the day. It is very clever at hiding. It adores gardeners who leave piles of debris around. You can tell if a slug is the beast who has been at your lettuce and other vegetables by the silvery trail it leaves behind. Slugs excrete a mucuslike substance that protects their soft bodies and provides a path for them to travel on.

REMEDIES

Clean up garden debris.

Find out where the slugs hide and kill them. You can do this act with a trowel or a sharp stick, but it is awful. You can also sprinkle them with salt and watch them die a slow death. I can't stand to do this, even to a slug. I much prefer dropping the creatures into a can of kerosene.

Set traps for slugs. Lay a board or boards in your garden, and when the sun is well up you will find the slugs hiding under the boards — scrape them off and kill them. Another trap is the beer trap. Sink small cans or saucers level with the ground and fill them with beer. Half water and half beer works as well and is less costly. The slugs are attracted by the beer and fall into it and drown. Slugs are also attracted to citrus fruits and will gather under them.

Sprinkle wood ashes or limestone around your plants. The slugs' soft bodies cannot tolerate the dry, sharp materials.

Get a toad or two toads. They think slugs are delicious.

A word about slugs and mulches. It is true that slugs hide under mulches. But that does not mean that a mulched garden is a slug heaven. My Maine farmer friend has a huge garden and never mulches an inch of it. Yet his garden is beset by slugs as often as mine is. It is clear to me now that slugs are a fact of life (or strife) in any kind of a garden, so I shall go right on mulching.

ANIMALS

Rabbits
Wild rabbits will consider that you planted your lettuce and many other vegetables solely for their benefit.

REMEDIES
Enclose your garden with a chicken-wire fence at least 30 inches high.
Make long wire cages to fit over lettuce and other crops rabbits eat.
Sprinkle dried bloodmeal around plants.
Intercrop with onions.

Gophers
Gophers can tunnel into your garden and devastate it in no time at all.

REMEDIES

Gophers can be flooded out of their burrows or trapped in specially made gopher traps.

There is now available at many garden centers a little windmill called Klippity-Klop. It sets up a vibration in the ground which gophers cannot stand. As a result, they tunnel in the opposite direction.

Woodchucks

I don't really know what you do about woodchucks. I do know they can level a lettuce patch as the main course and then go on to all your other vegetables for dessert.

REMEDIES

Last summer our neighbor tried to "live trap" a woodchuck. He caught a skunk. He tried again. He caught a possum. He never caught the woodchuck and he lost his entire lettuce crop. Maybe you would have better luck.

As for fences, woodchucks can burrow under them and climb them. You can line the bottom of a wire fence with hardware cloth to foil the burrowing. Ruth Stout devised a wire fence with a floppy wire top which discouraged the woodchucks from climbing over it. It is difficult to make a fence that is woodchuckproof.

Cats and Dogs

I am sure your own cats and dogs are too well trained to set a paw in your vegetable garden. Neighbors' pets present another problem, one that can cause an uneasy social climate with a forecast of hot-weather words to follow. I don't think neighbors' dogs are as much of a problem as their cats. The dogs I have dealt with are quick to take the strong hints I have given them to stay out of our yard. Cats are something else again. Fences don't bother them and they don't just run through a garden, they dig in it, and once they find a favorite spot they keep coming back to it. The first year we moved to our present home, I planted a new garden. No sooner did the seedlings come up than they were dug up. My lettuce patch became *the* place to dig and only a half-dozen or so seedlings survived the attack. I replanted, but the seeds never had a chance to germinate.

I had no idea what was causing such havoc in my lettuce patch, but I was hopping mad. I began to watch my garden, lurking around it at all hours of the day and some at night. It paid off. I caught our neighbor's black and white tom-cat, the size of a small lynx, making the dirt and seedlings fly to a fare-thee-well. Now that I had discovered the culprit, what was I to do? I would certainly have to speak to the cat's owner, but what would I say? Tell him to keep his cat in the house? Tie it up outside? Train it to stay in his yard? I put off speaking to my neighbor and resorted to throwing things at the cat. It didn't work. Old tom had found *his* place to dig and I could go fly a kite for all he cared. I became so cross over the cat problem that my family began avoiding me. The day I decided to speak to our neighbor, my husband solved the whole miserable matter. He gave me an eight-month-old poodle puppy named Percy. He was larger than the tom-cat and he quickly learned that his main obligation to his mistress was to keep the neighbor's cat, and all other cats, out of her garden.

If you have a cat digging in your garden and no dog like Percy, go have a nice friendly chat with your neighbor.

DROUGHT

Hot, dry, rainless weather is surely an enemy of lettuce and all other vege-tables. Without water the soil cannot spread its nutrients. A plant's nour-ishment is carried by water up through its stalk to its leaves. In dry weather you need to water the wilting leaves as well as the soil. It was once believed that you should never water your garden at midday, but that is one more old gardener's tale. Now it is believed that plants benefit from being watered when the sun is high to prevent the leaf-wilt that slows down and can have an adverse effect on plant growth. I water my wilting vegetables at noon, using a hose with a fine spray. My lettuce and other salad greens, in particular, perk up considerably.

The best protection for root systems in time of drought is a mulch from 6 to 8 inches deep. Should the drought persist, feel under the mulch to see if the ground has dried out. If it has, give your garden a good, deep soaking once a week.

Chapter Five

A Salad Green Seminar

Salad greens are all those other worthy leafy vegetables that can add extra zest to salads, either by themselves or tossed in with lettuce. This is not to dismiss lettuce salads, not at all — they often get gold stars in my salad roster. But as a salad buff, I enjoy creating salads that include additional appeals to taste, eye, and texture.

The following is a list of my favorite greens. Unless I advise otherwise, they have the same basic growing requirements that lettuce has. To keep your leafy greens going, make small sowings every 2 to 3 weeks during their specified growing periods. If you prefer, you can make successive plantings with plants instead of seeds, as you can do with "standby lettuce." Troubles (diseases and pests) are only mentioned when they are serious enough to call to your attention. I have given the directions for planting salad greens in rows, but you can also plant them in groups or broadcast them, as I have suggested for lettuce. Just be sure you space the plants according to their individual requirements.

CELERY

This is not the easiest salad green for the backyard gardener to grow but it is a rewarding one. You can feel proud of yourself if you grow good celery. I think celery makes a splendid salad as the only star and it can also play an important supporting role in mixed salads.

How to Grow

Celery needs a rich, moist soil and will do especially well in soil that has been mixed with equal parts of rotted manure. Frequent watering and heavy mulching are musts. Celery has a small, shallow root system and it can easily fall victim to drying out and being overtaken by weeds.

You can grow celery from seed or you can buy plants. Plants may be set out as soon as the danger of frost has passed. Seeds can be sown outdoors about 10 days before the last expected frost. To plant seeds, soak overnight and sow thinly in rows 2 feet apart. Barely cover the seeds with a fine soil. Thin the plants to stand 6 to 8 inches apart in the rows.

Celery can be started indoors 10 to 12 weeks before setting the plants in the garden. Use a "soil-less soil" (see page 80) and press the seeds, 8 seeds per inch, into the medium. Keep them moist and cool (65° F.). Transplant 3-inch plants into the garden and fertilize well.

BLANCHING

I have never tried blanching celery as it seems too much trouble and I like the look of green celery. Besides, green celery is better for you — it is higher in vitamins than the blanched. Now that the lecture is over, here is how you blanch celery: In summer, when the plants are 1 foot tall you must protect them from the sun so that they will turn white. To do this, place 1-foot boards, bunches of newspaper, or black plastic around each stalk, or hill up around the plants with soil, leaving 6 to 8 inches of the leafy top exposed. You will have blanched celery in about twelve days.

HARVESTING

Nearly any time. I find that celery is good at all stages of its growth. Cut single stalks or pull up the entire plant and cut off the roots.

TROUBLES

Chlorosis or yellow foliage. Makes celery plants turn yellow and bitter and stunts their growth. Remedy: Plant nonchlorotic varieties.

Blight. Foliage gets spotted and turns yellowish. Remedies: Rotate site. Stay out of celery patch when plants are wet.

VARIETIES

Beacon	100 days	Nonchlorotic. Early, short, dark green.
Summer Pascal	115 days	A slow-bolter with thick green stems.
Nichols French Dinant	100 days	Fuller flavor than common celery. Resists light frosts.

Plant midseason for fall
and winter harvest. Green,
stringless.

CELTUCE   80 DAYS

I discovered this green last year and I love it. Celtuce tastes like what its name says it is — a combination of celery and lettuce. Actually, it belongs to the lettuce family and looks like romaine. It is four times higher in vitamin C than head lettuce.

How to Grow

Grow celtuce exactly as you grow lettuce. It is a fast grower and does not need to be started indoors; it can be sown directly in the garden several weeks before the last expected frost. Plant again in midsummer for a fall crop.

Celtuce

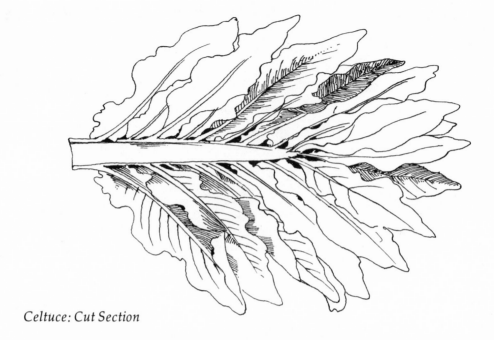

Celtuce: Cut Section

Sow seeds thinly in rows 1 foot apart, ¼ inch deep. Thin the plants to stand 15 inches apart in the row.

HARVESTING

Use the thinnings in salads and begin picking the leaves of the more mature plants when they are about 5 inches high. When the plants are 8 inches tall, cut the entire plant off at the base and use the heart sliced in salads. Be sure you peel off the outer skin before you use the stalk. Celtuce is a cut-and-come-again vegetable. If you leave its stump in the ground it will grow new shoots.

TROUBLES

Same as lettuce.

Also called "succory," chicory is often confused with endive and escarole (which are the same plant). The chicory you buy in the market is really curly endive. To further confuse matters, the four varieties of chicory I recommend you try are very different plants. First, there is the popular Italian Radichetta (also called Asparagus chicory), whose dark green leaves are used for spring salads. Second, Sugarhat, a green widely grown in Europe but a relatively new variety of chicory in this country, is both heat and frost resistant, self-blanching, and truly delicious whether raw or cooked. Third, there is Witloof chicory, a hefty green that is grown for its roots, which are forced in the fall to produce *chicons*, or Belgian or French endive, the caviar of salad vegetables. Finally, there is Rossa de Verona, a beautiful red-leaved chicory with a bitter flavor to use when you want to sharpen up bland greens.

RADICHETTA   65 DAYS

HOW TO GROW
Radichetta is a cool-weather vegetable and should be planted in early spring as soon as the ground can be worked. Plant it again in midsummer for a fall harvest.

Sow seeds thinly in rows 1 foot apart, ¼ inch deep. Thin the plants to stand 15 inches apart in the row.

HARVESTING
Pick the young leaves for Italian salads and slice the young shoots for mixed salads. You can also boil the stalks, which taste mildly like asparagus.

SUGARHAT   86 DAYS
Sugarhat is very demanding about being watered and mulched. Plant it early in the spring as soon as the ground can be worked. Sow seeds in rows 1 foot apart, ¼ inch deep. Sow again in midsummer for a fall harvest. The first

year I planted Sugarhat for a fall harvest, I protected it with a good mulch when the weather turned cold. We had several days and nights when the temperature went down to 10° F. and I was sure the Sugarhat was done for. When I went out to inspect it, the outside leaves were black and quite dreadful-looking. But, lo and behold, when I peeled them off the inside leaves were unharmed and blanched nearly white. When I tasted them they were tender and tangy. I harvested my last head of Sugarhat in January and could have kept on harvesting until spring had I planted enough to last until then.

HARVESTING
Pull the entire head or pick the leaves as you need them. I like the inner leaves the best.

Witloof Chicory (Belgian Endive)   110 days
The following how-to might sound like a lot of trouble. It isn't, once you get the hang of it. When you eat your first home-grown, plump Belgian endive, you'll be so proud of yourself you won't give the effort it took to grow it a second thought.

Late spring is the time to plant Witloof chicory so that by fall there will be large leafy plants with good healthy roots for forcing indoors.

Sow the seeds in rows 18 to 24 inches apart, ¼ inch deep. Thin the plants to stand 4 to 6 inches apart in the row and use the thinnings in a salad for a nippy taste. After two months, fertilize the plants.

HARVESTING
In September, or before the first hard frost, when the leaves of the chicory have wilted, dig up the roots, being careful not to split them. Shake off the dirt, cut the tops off the plants, leaving 2 inches of the stalk. If you aren't going to force them right away, store them in a cool place. If you have room in your refrigerator, store them in it. It is important that the roots do not freeze — throw them away if they do.

The ideal place to force the roots is in a cool cellar or room where the temperature is between 50° and 60° F. When you are ready to force a set of roots, trim each root to the same length — about 8 inches is best.

Put 2 inches of soil into a wooden box, tub, or plastic pail which is at least 18 inches deep. Stand the roots up in the soil so that they nearly touch each other, about 1 inch apart. Fill the container with enough soil to cover the roots. Water thoroughly.

Fill the container to the top with dry sand — lugging the sand is the hardest part of the whole procedure — and cover the container with a damp cloth or burlap.

In about three weeks, check to see if the *chicons* (endive heads) are poking up through the surface of the sand. If they are, it is time to pick Belgian endive! Remove the top layer of sand and cut the endive heads off at their roots. Replace the sand and force the roots a second time. The second growth does not produce such tight, plump heads as the first, but they are just as tender and tasty. Some people say they can force the roots a third time. I've never tried to.

To keep supplied with Belgian endive, I use two containers. Two weeks after I have picked the heads from the first container and am forcing the roots a second time, I start another set of roots in the other container.

Rossa de Verona   85 days

HOW TO GROW
Plant in midsummer exactly like Witloof chicory for a light fall harvest. Mulch the plants for wintering over until the following spring, when the plants should be cut back to 2 to 3 inches above the ground. They will then produce rosettes of reddish-green leaves which turn a bright red in the fall.

HARVESTING
Pick the small rosette heads when they reach the size of a tennis ball. The roots of Rossa de Verona can be forced in the same manner as Witloof chicory roots.

CHINESE CABBAGE

A member of the cabbage family, this vegetable looks like a cross between cabbage and celery and is sometimes called celery cabbage or long cabbage. Chinese cabbage has a pleasant tartness to it and a mild celery taste. Its leaves are good in mixed green salads and, when chopped, make a superior slaw. When cooked, Chinese cabbage has a milder taste than ordinary cabbage. It is used extensively in Oriental dishes and is a real treat cooked and served with a hollandaise sauce.

How to Grow

Chinese cabbage likes a rich, moist, loamy soil. It is strictly a cool-weather crop, so wait until mid-July to plant it for a fall harvest. It can withstand light frosts when protected by a light mulch. Planting Chinese cabbage in the spring is chancy, as it bolts and goes to seed quickly in hot weather.

Chinese cabbage is one of my favorite vegetables, and I have started a fast-maturing variety indoors 4 to 6 weeks before the last frost and transplanted it into my garden around the time of the last frost. I harvested it before the hot weather arrived.

Sow seeds thinly in rows 20 inches apart and ½ inch deep. Thin plants to stand 1 foot apart in the row. In transplanting thinnings, keep as much soil as possible around the roots. Feed the plants twice during the growing season with a fertilizer high in nitrogen, such as blood meal, bone meal, or dried manure. Water the plants well in hot weather.

HARVESTING

You can cut the cylindrical heads before they are completely mature. Discard the outer leaves and slice the tender, blanched inner leaves into your salads.

TROUBLES

The worst I've found are slugs. Aphids and cabbage worms can be a problem, too. To control cabbage worms, sprinkle the plants daily with salt water before they form heads.

VARIETIES

Crispy Choy	45 days	Tastes more like celery than the other varieties.
Burpee Hybrid	75 days	Grows 13 inches high, 8 inches across. Inner leaves blanch nearly white.
Michihli	78 days	Heads grow 18 inches tall. Has sweet and spicy flavor.
Stokes Hybrids:		
Springtime	60 days	Slow bolting, for spring planting in cool-weather areas.
Summertime	70 days	A later-maturing variety for fall harvest.
Wintertime	80 days	For late September, early October harvests. Good variety for storing.

Corn Salad

CORN SALAD

Whether you call corn salad "field salad," "fetticus," or "lamb's lettuce" (the French call it *mâches*), I urge you to put it on your salad green must list. Corn salad is a pretty plant with dark green, spoon-shaped leaves that form a rosette. It has a mild, sweet (slightly flowery) flavor with a texture like butterhead lettuce. You can leave it in the ground for months and it never turns bitter or loses its flavor. I like corn salad best when combined with sharper greens or with such root vegetables as beets, radishes, and carrots; it is delicious when cooked like spinach.

Corn salad bolts quickly in heat but it is hardy enough to withstand frost and will last through the winter if protected by a mulch. As I write this on a snowy January day, there are a dozen or so tiny corn salad plants under a light salt hay mulch and four inches of snow in my garden. In spring I will uncover them so they can grow into mature plants for April and May salads.

How to Grow

Corn salad is grown like lettuce except that it does not transplant well and seeds should be sown directly in the ground where the plants are to grow. Sow in early spring as soon as the ground is workable in rows 1 foot apart, ¼ inch deep. Thin plants to stand 10 to 12 inches apart in the row. Sow in midsummer for a fall crop, then again 2 to 4 weeks before the last frost to have plants to carry over through the winter.

Harvesting
Slice the plant off at its base or pick the leaves as you need them. Repeated picking stimulates new growth. I have harvested the outer leaves in less than a month without damaging the plants' growth.

Varieties

Stokes Corn Salad	45 days	Good for spring, late summer, and fall plantings.
Thompson & Morgan's Verte de Cambrai	60 days	Cool-weather variety. Very frost hardy.

DANDELION   95 DAYS

Grow dandelion in your garden when you can weed it out of your lawn or pick it almost anywhere in spring? Only if you have the room for it. Cultivated dandelion is quite different from the wild variety. It has larger and thicker leaves, a slower rate of growth, and it is not as prolific. Whether cultivated or wild, dandelion is good for you. It is an excellent source of vitamin A and it contains calcium and potassium.

How to Grow
Sow seeds in midspring, 2 seeds per inch in rows 9 inches apart, ¼ inch deep. Thin plants to stand 9 inches apart in the row. Keep the plants well watered to prevent bolting. You can improve the flavor of cultivated dandelion by tying the outer leaves together to blanch the hearts. Never let your dandelion flower — it will take over the garden if you do.

HARVESTING

Pick the fresh new leaves regularly or pull the entire plant and chop the inner leaves raw into your salads.

ENDIVE AND ESCAROLE

Endive and escarole are the same plant. The curly-leaved variety is called endive and the broad-leaved variety is called escarole. They make excellent salad greens but are a little bitter and are best mixed with blander greens. As they mature, the inner leaves blanch and become sweet and mild tasting.

HOW TO GROW

Plant in early spring and again in early summer for a fall crop. In the fall under a light mulch, the plants will last 2 to 3 weeks after the lettuce has gone. For a spring planting, start indoors or in a coldframe 6 to 8 weeks before the last expected frost and transplant into the garden around the date of the last frost.

For an early spring salad extra, pull mature plants up by the roots in the fall, leaving a ball of soil around them. Store (do not plant) the plants in a coldframe or other cool place where they will get light but will not freeze. In early spring, place the plants in the garden and, by the end of April, enjoy endive-escarole salads.

Sow seeds in rows 1 foot apart, ¼ inch deep. Thin plants to stand 16 to 18 inches apart in the row. Although the plants will do some self-blanching on their own, you can further the blanching of the hearts by tying the outer leaves loosely together over the top of the plants. Blanching takes about two weeks. When the plants begin to mature, don't let water collect in the hearts or they will rot. If you have tied up the leaves and there has been a heavy rain, untie them and let them dry out, then tie them up again.

HARVESTING

Pick the heads before they are completely mature. The inner leaves are the best, as the outer leaves tend to be tough and bitter.

Escarole Leaf

VARIETIES

Green, Curled Endive	90 days	Curled, fringed leaves. Plants grow to 16 to 18 inches in diameter.
Salad King Endive	98 days	Good heat- and frost-resistant endive.
Broad-Leaved Batavian Escarole	90 days	Large, lettucelike leaves.

FENNEL, SWEET FLORENCE   90 DAYS

Sweet fennel has a mild anise flavor combined with a mellow celery taste. It is a rather odd-looking annual plant (not to be confused with the herb or common fennel). It grows a thick, bulblike stalk topped by spreading, feathery leaves. Both the leaves and stalks are usable. The stalks may be eaten raw or cooked.

How to Grow

Sow in spring after the danger of frost has passed and again in midsummer in rows 18 inches apart. Barely cover seeds with soil. Thin the plants to stand 6 inches apart in the row. The stalks can be blanched when they are half-grown by hilling up around them with soil.

Harvesting

Cut leaves any time and cut stalks before they grow too large and become tough and stringy.

KALE

Kale is a nonheading variety of cabbage. I used to think kale was only good boiled, but I have since discovered that its leaves used raw give salads a mild cabbage taste and good green looks.

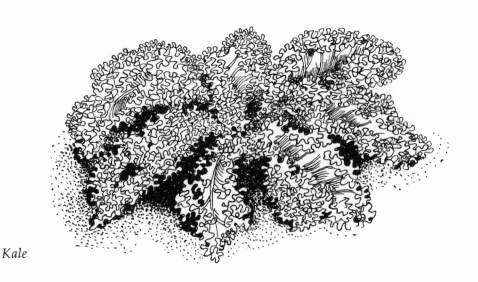

Kale

Kale doesn't like heat at all, but it is so hardy it can last all winter when protected with a mulch. Plant kale in early spring, 4 weeks before the last frost, and again in midsummer and late summer for a fall and winter crop.

Sow seeds in well-limed soil in rows 20 inches apart, ½ inch deep. When the plants are 4 inches high, thin them to stand 16 inches apart in the row. Fertilize the plants halfway through the growing season. Kale has shallow roots and needs to be mulched, particularly in hot weather.

Harvesting

Pick the entire plant before it is fully mature, or pick the outer leaves, which allows new ones to grow.

Troubles

See Chinese cabbage.

Varieties

Dwarf Siberian	65 days	Grayish, plumelike leaves spread to 36 inches.
Green Curled Scotch	55 days	Yellow-green leaves with white ribs. Eat young leaves like lettuce.
Dwarf Blue Curled	60 days	Dark blue-green leaves. A compact variety. Particularly good for fall and winter crops.
Blue Leaf	110 days	Very hardy.

MUSTARD

I don't like cooked mustard greens so I only grow a half-dozen mustard plants to use in my salads when I want to perk them up. Mustard is full of vitamin A and also contains vitamin B, calcium, iron, and phosphorus. It is also so easy to grow that you can do it with your green thumb tied behind your back.

How to Grow

Plant mustard in early spring as soon as the ground is workable and again in midsummer for a fall crop. Don't bother with a summer crop, as mustard turns bitter in hot weather. I never plant it after mid-April.

Sow seeds in rows 1 foot apart, ¼ inch deep. Thin the plants to stand 8 inches apart in the row. Don't let the soil dry out — thorough watering is a mustard must.

Harvesting

Pick mustard leaves when the plants are only 25 days old, or about 3 to 4 inches tall. With mustard, the more you pick it the more it grows, and the longer it grows the spicier it gets. Be careful not to let mustard flower and go to seed, as it will turn up all over your garden like a bothersome weed next spring.

Varieties

Tendergreen	25 days	Dark green leaves are thick and taste like spinach, only spicier.
Ostrich Plume	35 days	Plumed, dark green leaves, slow to bolt. Difficult to clean.

PURSLANE   45 DAYS

For years the French have cultivated a large-leaved, upright plant which is a variation of the sprawling purslane we weed out of our lawns and gardens. The French call their plant *pourpier* and use the spatula-shaped leaves with a light dressing to make a French chef's gourmet salad delight. I grew some purslane last year and found it to have an unusual and piquant flavor, quite delicious. Purslane is another healthy green — it contains large amounts of iron.

Sow seeds from early spring to fall in rows 10 inches apart, ½ inch deep. Thin plants to stand 6 inches apart in the row.

Harvesting

Pick leaves and stems as needed. Be sure to wash, dry, and chill the leaves before using.

SORREL   45 DAYS

In the wild, sorrel is known as a weed most commonly called "sour grass" and "dock" — of which there are many varieties. Seeds for home growing have been developed to produce larger and broader leaves with a milder flavor than the wild varieties. (The only source I have found for seeds is the De Giorgi Seed Company, which sells Mammoth Lyon Sorrel.) A few chopped leaves of sorrel can add a lot of sock to an otherwise bland salad.

How to Grow

Get a clump from a friend, buy a plant, or sow seeds in early spring as soon as the ground is workable. Make rows 1 foot apart and sow seeds ¼ inch deep. Thin plants to stand 8 inches apart in the row. (One or two plants should be sufficient.) Sorrel is a perennial and should be divided every other year. Water sorrel well in hot weather.

Harvesting

Pick the outside leaves as you need them (this allows the clump to spread). Leaves will get bitter if the plant is allowed to flower, so keep cutting off the flower stalks.

Troubles

Be on the watch for slugs.

Spinach

SPINACH

There have been quite a few spinach disasters in my vegetable garden. I do not take the blame. I place it firmly on the weather, which can turn May into July to make my spinach bolt faster than a jack rabbit can run. Now, thanks to the improved varieties of spinach and the heat-resistant spinach substitutes, I have had a lot fewer failures. Anyway, I keep trying — for me, spinach is the king of salad greens.

If possible, grow spinach in the part of your garden which gets the most shade in ground well fed with nitrogen fertilizer. Sow seeds in early spring, 4 to 6 weeks before the last frost in rows 1 foot apart, ½ inch deep. Firm the ground after planting and keep it well watered. Thin seedlings to stand 4 inches apart in the row and transplant seedlings to make a new row. Plant again in midsummer for a fall harvest. A cold-resistant variety can be mulched to winter over until spring to provide you with an early crop.

Harvesting

While spinach is still young, pull every other plant or pick the outer leaves and leave the center intact to grow new leaves.

Troubles

Aphids.

Downy mildew and spinach yellows are found mostly on fall crops. Pull up affected plants and destroy them.

Varieties

Bloomsdale Long Standing	48 days	Slow to bolt, compact plants, dark green, crinkled leaves.
America	50 days	Slow to bolt. Savoyed, dark green leaves.
Avon Hybrid	44 days	New, improved, slow-bolting variety. Blight and mildew resistant. For fall harvest.
Cleanleaf	45 days	Emerald green leaves. Plants grow upright, stay clean. A cool-weather variety.
Cold Resistant Savoy	45 days	Blight, heat, and frost resistant. Will winter over.

SPINACH SUBSTITUTES

These are greens that look and taste like spinach but aren't really spinach. Thank goodness for them — they are near to miraculous the way they keep going on and on throughout the summer as if the weather couldn't get hot enough for them.

MALABAR OR CLIMBING SPINACH   70 DAYS

This is an annual plant that produces enormous amounts of bright green, smooth leaves on vines which grow to 4 feet high and need to be supported.

HOW TO GROW

Malabar spinach is not frost resistant, so plant it in spring after the danger of frost has passed. Sow 3 to 4 seeds per foot, in rows 12 to 18 inches apart, 1 inch deep. Thin plants to stand 1 foot apart in the row. You can start Malabar spinach indoors one month before the last expected frost and transplant it into your garden after the last frost.

HARVESTING

Pick young leaves as you need them, count ten, and there will be new leaves growing to replace the harvested ones.

NEW ZEALAND OR SPREADING SPINACH   70 DAYS

This is such a heat-resistant green that it can be harvested all summer. It has small, thick, "fleshy" (a seed catalog word) leaves with tender branch tips.

HOW TO GROW

New Zealand spinach takes a long time to germinate, so soak the seeds 24 hours before planting them. After the danger of frost has passed, sow seeds 1 to the inch in rows 4 feet apart, 1 inch deep. Thin plants to stand 1 to 2 feet apart in the row. I find that one planting in the spring is enough to last me all summer. Side-dress the plants with a nitrogen fertilizer every 3 weeks and water well. You can start New Zealand spinach indoors in individual containers or peat pots 6 weeks before the last frost. Like a beet seed, each seed of New Zealand contains several seeds and the seedlings come up in clusters. Keep only one seedling to a container by snipping off the extras. Transplant the seedlings into the garden after the last frost. Once established, this "spinach" spreads out 3 to 5 feet in every direction.

HARVESTING
Cut 3 to 4 inches off each branch tip. For the best flavor, do not pick the small seedpod next to the main stem.

TAMPALA OR FORDHOOK SPINACH
Also called "Chinese spinach," Tampala is another dependable green for summer growing. It is easy to raise and can reach a height of 3 feet.

HOW TO GROW
Sow seeds directly in the garden after the danger of frost has passed, 2 seeds to the inch, ¼ inch deep, in rows 8 inches apart. Thin plants to stand 4 inches apart in the row.

HARVESTING
For the tenderest Tampala greens, pick 4 to 5 inches off the tips of the plants when the plants are 6 inches high.

SPINACH BEET OR LEAF BEET   50 DAYS
This plant is similar to Swiss chard. It grows large reddish tops that look very pretty when planted next to a dark green spinach. According to the seed catalog, spinach beet is similar to the wild beets the Romans cultivated for their leafy tops. The "greens" are usually cooked, but I like to use them chopped up in mixed green salads.

HOW TO GROW

Soak seeds 24 hours before planting. Sow in early spring as soon as the ground is workable, in rows 9 inches apart, ½ inch deep. Thin the plants to stand 3 inches apart in the row. If the weather turns hot and you are not a mulcher, be sure to keep the seedlings well watered.

HARVESTING

Pick the young leaves as you need them and new leaves will keep coming.

Chapter Six

Salad Herbs
and Other Enhancements

HERBS ARE my salad bowl's magicians. They can transform a so-so salad into one that is mellow, sharp, delicate, and even mysterious. They can imitate the flavor of vegetables in the most subtle way. By adding herbs to your dressings as well as to your salads, you can make a myriad of tastes. But beware — I have, on occasion, added too many herbs and other vegetables and ended up with an inedible concoction I had to throw on my compost heap.

You can use herbs fresh, or dry them or freeze them. (Use twice as much fresh or frozen as you would dried herbs.) Dry them by hanging small bunches by their stems in an airy place. When they are thoroughly dried out, crush the leaves between your fingers and store them in airtight bottles and label them. If you like a combination of herbs, dry and store a salad mix of your favorites. Freeze herbs by washing a small bunch and drying them between paper towels or in a salad spinner. Then put them in a plastic bag, tie it closed, and store in the freezer. Don't forget to tag each bag.

You can be very fancy with the way you grow your salad herbs or you can grow them the way I do — rather casually, wherever I have the room for them. One year I grew my herbs in a circle in the middle of my vegetable garden, but as I began to grow more kinds of herbs, I needed more room. So now, in addition to the circle, I grow them in and around my lettuce and other salad greens, in my flower garden, and in several pots on my patio.

It is not true that herbs like a poor soil. The majority of them like and need as good a soil as vegetables do.

Herb seeds and plants are available at garden centers and some grocery and hardware stores. You can also order them from seed catalogs.

Here are the herbs and other plants I like to season my salads with.

ANISE (ANNUAL, SELF-SOWING)   75 DAYS

For a mild licorice taste, add anise to your salads.

Anise can be planted around the date of the last frost. It needs full sun.

Sow seeds ¼ inch deep and space the plants 6 inches apart. The plants grow to a height of 18 inches and should be supported.

Harvesting
Pick the young leaves as you need them.

BASIL, SWEET GREEN (ANNUAL)   80 DAYS

An extremely aromatic plant used mostly with tomatoes, but also good in green salads when used sparingly.

How to Grow
Sow in the garden after the danger of frost has passed or start indoors 6 to 8 weeks before the last frost. Basil likes sun but will do all right in partial shade.

Sow seeds ¼ inch deep and space plants 6 inches apart. If your soil is very rich, space plants 10 inches apart. Basil roots quickly in water and then can be transplanted into the garden. I keep my basil going all summer by this method.

Harvesting
Pick the leaves as you need them and pinch out the flower buds to keep the plants bushy.

BASIL, PURPLE (ANNUAL)   80 DAYS

This is a larger, less aromatic herb than green basil. I use it in my salads for its color. If you add purple and green basil to vinegar, you will have a light pink vinegar which you can use for tossed green salads or for tomatoes.

How to Grow
Grow like green basil and space plants 15 inches apart.

HARVESTING
Same as green basil.

CHERVIL (BIENNIAL, BUT TREAT AS AN ANNUAL) 75 DAYS

This herb looks like parsley and tastes like parsley with a little fennel thrown in for a licorice taste. (Actually, it is related to parsley.) It makes a good substitute for lettuce in sandwiches.

How to Grow
Chervil prefers semishade and does not do well in heat. It is best to plant it for a spring and fall crop.

Sow seeds as soon as the ground is workable, ⅛ inch deep. Space plants 6 inches apart.

HARVESTING
Pick the young leaves as you need them.

CHIVES (PERENNIAL)   80 DAYS

Chives belong to the onion family and can be used in place of onions in your salads for a change of pace.

How to Grow
The easiest way is to buy a plant from your local grocery store or super-market. Cut the foliage back and transplant the roots into a sunny spot after all danger of frost has passed.

To grow chives from seeds: sow them in early spring several weeks before the last expected frost. Sow seeds ¼ inch deep and thin the plants to stand in clumps of 6 seedlings each. The following spring, thin the clumps to stand 6 inches apart. Chives should be divided every year. One large clump of chives should be enough to last all season.

Snip tops with scissors as you need them. If your chives bloom, allow the blossoms to wither, then cut down the entire plant to about 3 inches above the ground; they will grow up quickly again.

Chives freeze well. Cut or chop them into small pieces and put them in a plastic container and freeze them. Very handy.

CHIVES, GARLIC (PERENNIAL)   80 DAYS

Garlic chives resemble the common chives except that the leaves are flat instead of tubular and they have a mild garlic taste. Both the white, starlike flowers and the stems are good in salads, particularly spinach salads.

HOW TO GROW
Grow like common chives.

HARVESTING
Cut often to keep the stems tender.

CRESS, CURLED (ANNUAL)   25 DAYS

Better known as "peppergrass," this is an odd-tasting, spicy plant with bright green, delicate leaves. If you have never tried peppergrass, you're in for a new taste thrill.

HOW TO GROW
Broadcast seeds in early spring, 2 weeks before the last frost, and cover lightly with soil. Thin plants to 6 inches apart. As peppergrass goes to seed quickly, make new sowings every 2 weeks. Cress doesn't like summer heat, so plant it in semishade when the weather turns hot and use it up fast.

HARVESTING
Pick in about 2 weeks and before it flowers.

Anise

Dill

CRESS, UPLAND (BIENNIAL BEST GROWN AS AN ANNUAL)   25 DAYS

This cress looks and tastes like its relative watercress, except that it is a larger plant — 18 inches high and 10 inches wide. It has a milder taste than peppergrass. If you don't have a brook to grow watercress in, both upland cress and peppergrass are good substitutes.

How to Grow

Same as peppergrass. In the late fall, I protect my upland cress with mulch to winter over for early spring salads.

Harvesting

You can pick upland cress 10 days after it is planted or when it is 3 inches high.

DILL (ANNUAL)   70 DAYS

I have so many uses for dill that I can't imagine my culinary life without it. A lettuce salad with lots and lots of chopped fresh dill plus oil and vinegar and a little salt is almost too good to be true.

How to Grow

Dill likes sun and does best in good soil, so dig a little fertilizer into the ground before you plant it. Once planted, dill is likely to come up any old place in your garden, as it is a prolific self-sower. Don't try to transplant your wandering dill back to where you want it to be — dill is tap-rooted and won't transplant well.

Sow seeds in spring after the danger of frost has passed, ¼ inch deep. Grow dill in clumps to keep the 3-foot mature plants from falling over, or grow in rows 1 foot apart and tie them up to bamboo stakes. Reseed every 3 weeks.

Harvesting
Pick leaves at any stage of growth.

GARLIC (BULB)   100 DAYS

I wonder if all owners of wooden salad bowls are divided between those who rub the inside of the bowl with a cut clove of garlic and those who consider that to be a barbarian practice? My stand is that if you like garlic in your salads, add it any way you choose to.

With garlic so available and inexpensive, why bother to grow it? For one thing, it's handy to have your own fresh garlic, and for another, garlic is an excellent natural bug repellent.

How to Grow
Separate cloves of garlic sets and plant them in early spring as soon as the ground is workable. You can use the garlic you buy in the market, but this is chancy, as it is not as fresh as the sets you buy from seed catalogs and in garden centers. Plant the cloves 4 inches apart with the tip of the clove 2 inches below the surface of the soil. Rows should be 1 foot apart. When the flower heads bloom, pinch them off to allow the bulbs to develop.

Harvesting
Snip the stems of garlic and use them like chives. When the tops turn yellow and tip over, pull up the bulbs, clean off the loose skin, and trim the roots of the bulb close to the base. You can tie garlic in bunches or be fancy and plait the stems and hang them in your kitchen for a professional look. Garlic may also be stored loose like onions.

LEMON BALM (HARDY PERENNIAL)   60 DAYS

Adding lemon balm leaves to your salad is a fine thing to do on a hot summer's night; lemon balm has a delightfully cool and refreshing taste. Add it to your iced tea as well and forget the heat.

How to Grow

Buy plants, or sow seeds in the spring as soon as the ground is workable. Lemon balm prefers sun but will also do well in semishade.

Sow seeds ⅛ inch deep and space the plants 8 inches apart. After the balm flowers, the runners can be used to produce new plants. Divide the plants every two years. Allow your lemon balm to go through the winter with its leaves on.

Harvesting

Pick the young, fresh leaves as you need them.

LOVAGE (PERENNIAL)   40 DAYS

Watch out for lovage! It is extremely pungent and tastes like a combination of curry and celery. A few leaves are enough to flavor a salad. Lovage adds a lot to potato salad.

How to Grow

Lovage likes full sun and should be planted in late summer or fall.

Sow seeds ⅛ inch deep and space plants 2 feet apart. One plant of lovage is quite ample. You can also propagate it by dividing the roots in spring and fall. Lovage will grow to a height of 5 to 7 feet if it is not cut back. To keep it bushy, cut off the flower stalks in the spring.

Harvesting

Pick young leaves as you need them.

MARJORAM, SWEET (PERENNIAL BEST TREATED AS AN ANNUAL)   45 DAYS

The old reliable, all-around herb, used to flavor soups, stews, cheese dishes, sauces, and salads, and for making salad vinegar.

Sweet Marjoram

How to Grow

Marjoram likes sun and a dry soil. It can be planted in spring 2 weeks before the last frost, or started indoors in late winter and transplanted into the garden after the last frost.

Sow seeds ¼ inch deep and space plants 6 to 8 inches apart.

Harvesting
Pick leaves as needed.

Otherwise known as "wild marjoram," oregano has a stronger flavor than sweet marjoram and is used mainly to flavor Italian dishes. I like to sprinkle oregano leaves liberally on tossed green salads. With a simple dressing of oil, vinegar, salt, and pepper, it makes an unusual and delicious salad.

How to Grow
Oregano likes sun and well-drained soil. Sow seeds outdoors just after the last frost and barely cover the seeds with soil. Space plants 18 inches apart. Fertilize once a year and divide plants every two years. Oregano can be started indoors in winter and transplanted into the garden after the last frost. To keep the plants bushy, do not allow them to flower.

Harvesting
Pick leaves as you need them. For drying, cut the stems as the flowers begin to develop.

PARSLEY (BIENNIAL BEST GROWN AS AN ANNUAL)

Parsley is the emperor of vitamins A and C. One teaspoon will give you all you need of these vitamins for the next twenty-four hours. For flavoring my salads, I prefer the flat-leaved Italian variety and use curly parsley more as a garnish.

How to Grow
Parsley will do well in either full sun or partial shade. It can be planted in early spring as soon as the ground is workable. Sow seeds, which have been soaked for twenty-four hours in water, 1/4 inch deep and space the plants 6 inches apart. If you plant parsley in rows, the rows should be 1 foot apart. Watch out for weeds, which can smother the small, slow-growing plants.

Parsley can also be started indoors 6 to 8 weeks before the last frost. Mulch your parsley in the fall and it will last well into the cold weather.

HARVESTING

Pick outer leaves and sprigs as you need them and new growth will keep coming. Or pick a bunch of parsley, put it in a glass of cold water, and store it in the refrigerator.

VARIETIES

Moss Curled	75 days	Long-stemmed, grows upright.
Extra-Curled Dwarf	85 days	Low, compact plants.
Italian Dark	78 days	Flat, celerylike leaves, strong flavor.
Darki	77 days	Tight, curled leaves, cold resistant.

ROCAMBOLE (SELF-SOWING PERENNIAL)   100 DAYS

An onion related to garlic, rocambole is also known as "giant garlic" and "everlasting leek." It is a huge plant that grows to a height of 3 feet and produces large cloves and light green stalks with a mild garlicky flavor and scent. It is good for flavoring salads when you don't want the pungency of garlic.

HOW TO GROW

In early spring, plant the bulblets like onion sets and then watch the fascinating procedure of propagation. The mature plant grows a bulb filled with tiny bulblets at the top of its flowering stalk, making the plant look like a tropical bird with an exotic plumage. Soon the bulb bursts and the weight of the bulblets causes the stalk to bend to the ground; the bulblets drop off and replant themselves. The mature plant dies down and a month later starts to grow new green stems. Divide plants in the spring.

HARVESTING

In midsummer, harvest the clusters of bulblets when they start to separate. Use the new green stems like chives.

(A plant similar to rocambole in its unique method of propagation is Egyptian onion. It produces larger bulblets, which have a mild onion flavor rather than a garlic one. Its young green stalks are delicious chopped into salads.)

ROCKET (PERENNIAL)   50 DAYS

Whether you call this salad herb rocket (English), *roquette* (French), or *argula* (Italian), you should grow it. It is a most versatile herb which can be used to flavor salads or by itself with only oil as a dressing. The taste of its chardlike leaves has been likened to horseradish, mustard, and turnips.

How to Grow
Rocket needs sun. It can be planted in the early spring as soon as the ground is workable, and in midseason to last through the first frosts.

Sow seeds ¼ inch deep and space plants 8 inches apart. You can broadcast the seeds and let your rocket go where it wants to around the garden. I do it this way because I like the spicy aroma of the yellow flowers, which I let bloom so the plants will self-sow. (Rocket is a dependable self-sower.)

Harvesting
Use the leaves of the young plants. Rocket gets bitter as it matures. Keep cutting the plants back for new and tender growth.

SALAD BURNET (PERENNIAL BEST GROWN AS AN ANNUAL)   45 DAYS

A pretty, feathery herb with a cucumber flavor.

How to Grow
Salad burnet needs full sun. It can be planted around the date of the last frost or started indoors in late winter and transplanted into the garden after the last frost.

Salad Burnet

Sow seeds ⅛ inch deep and space plants 10 inches apart. During the second season, the old plants get tangled and matted and do not grow well, so it is best to replant it every year.

HARVESTING
Pick the young leaves before the plants flower. Cut back the plants to encourage new growth.

TARRAGON (PERENNIAL)   60 DAYS

Tarragon has a slightly anise flavor. It makes a superb vinegar for salads.

HOW TO GROW
You can't get real (French) tarragon from seed. What you get from seed is a Russian tarragon — a large plant with very little flavor. The thing to do is to buy a plant or find someone who will divide a plant and give you a clump.

Tarragon likes sun and good soil, so add a little fertilizer to the soil when you plant your tarragon. However, too much fertilizing can sap the taste from tarragon leaves, and too much watering will rot its roots.

HARVESTING
When the plant has stems about a foot long, you can begin cutting the leaves. In the fall, cut the plant down to 3 inches above the ground, then mulch it well. Divide tarragon every three years.

THYME (PERENNIAL)   50 DAYS

There are some fifteen varieties of thyme, from the caraway-scented to the lemon thymes. I think the best thyme for salads is common or French, a hardy shrub with tiny pointed leaves.

HOW TO GROW
Thyme needs full sun and can be grown from seeds or cuttings or by dividing plants. It can be planted in spring after the last frost or started indoors 8 to 10 weeks before the last frost.

Thyme

Sow seeds ⅛ inch deep and space the plants 8 inches apart. Keep the small plants watered and then don't worry about watering them again until there is a dry spell.

HARVESTING
Cut tops as you need them before the plants bloom.

FLOWERS FOR SALADS

Not everyone likes to eat flowers. I don't eat many flowers, but the ones I do eat, I eat in salads, although I have been known to nibble violets on early spring walks. A green salad with flowers is lovely to behold and a joy to taste (to use flowery words). Toss flower petals — at least two dozen in a salad for four — with greens and decorate the top with whole flowers. Serve with a light dressing and watch the expressions on your family's and friends' faces as astonishment gives way to delight and a new appreciation is shown for your salad-making finesse.

CALENDULA OR POT MARIGOLD (SELF-SOWING ANNUAL)
Calendula is an old-fashioned flower. My grandmother loved calendulas and her garden was bright with their yellow and orange flowers. She would be amazed at the many colors and varieties of calendula there are today. There are dwarf, double-flowered, and long-stemmed single flowers in flame, apricot, and new shades of orange and yellow. I grow several varieties in both my flower and vegetable gardens.

HOW TO GROW
Sow seeds in early spring as soon as the ground is workable. Space the plants 12 inches apart. Calendula likes sun but is not fussy about the soil. If you keep picking the flowers, the plants will bloom in late spring and keep blooming until after light frosts.

NASTURTIUM (ANNUAL)

An old standby for flower eaters, nasturtiums have the sharp taste of watercress — both are members of the mustard family. Nasturtiums come in stunning colors of light and dark reds, yellows, and oranges. Their sizes and flower types range from double-dwarf to single-flowered and tall-climbing. Plant them in your vegetable garden for color accents, to help prevent whitefly, and to attract aphids away from your vegetables.

HOW TO GROW

Nasturtiums like sun, are easy to grow from seed, and do well in most any soil. Don't feed your nasturtiums; it causes them to put out too many large leaves and few flowers. Sow seeds in spring after the danger of frost has passed in the place you want them to grow, as they do not transplant well. Space the plants 8 to 10 inches apart. If you keep picking the flowers they will keep blooming until frost. You can use both the flowers and the leaves in your salads.

Try Red Eating Selected, hot and spicy, from Thompson and Morgan.

VIOLETS (PERENNIAL)

Violets are full of vitamins A and C — nature's spring tonic to help you cheer up after the long winter. Wild or cultivated, the leaves, stems, and flowers are usable in salads. Peppy and sweet.

HOW TO GROW

Buy plants from your local garden center. The cultivated varieties come with ruby, blue, white, purple, and yellow flowers. Violets like sun and do best in a rich soil, deeply spaded and kept moist. If you transplant wild violets into your garden, plant them in soil with lots of humus in it and in semishade. All violets appreciate being mulched. The more you pick them, the more they bloom.

Try freezing the tender inner leaves of violets to use as a winter green to combine with crisp bacon and chopped hard-cooked eggs. Steam the leaves with a small amount of water for 10 minutes, let them cool, and store in freezer containers.

Chapter Seven

Lettuce
and Salad Greens Everywhere

IF YOU DON'T have enough room in your backyard, if you live in an apartment or mobile home, or if you are simply not up to the rigors and demands of backyard vegetable gardening, don't despair — you can still grow your own fresh lettuce and other salad greens. Outdoors, flower beds, borders, lawns, patios, porches, balconies, and terraces can be put to double use to produce fine crops for your salad bowl. Indoors, living rooms, spare rooms, kitchens, attics, cellars, enclosed porches, windowsills, and even closets can provide space to grow salad makings.

FLOWER BEDS, BORDERS, LAWNS

Lettuce and other salad greens are decorative plants as well as edible ones. Think of them in terms of textures and colors, as you do your flowers, and visualize the magical effect of a garden of bright flowers mixed with the many shades and shapes of edible leafy greens.

One of my favorite gardens is a tiny front yard enclosed by a picket fence and filled to its corners with flowers and vegetables growing together. Lettuce and other greens, chard, broccoli, cabbage, beans, eggplant, and zucchini flourish in their time amidst annual and perennial flowers. A cucumber and a morning glory climb a lamp post at the gate, while the short path to the house is edged with a mixed border of herbs and California poppies. On the porch, hanging baskets of cherry tomatoes and midget cucumbers produce lavishly in the afternoon sun. I met the owner of the garden one day and complimented her on her ingenuity and the beauty of her garden. She thanked me, then added, "I'm English, you see, and I like my bit of land to work for me and be lovely as well."

With this English gardening philosophy in mind, plant a border of red Ruby lettuce and lime green Black-Seeded Simpson to set off your spring bulbs. Border a path or edge a flower bed with cress, dark green curled parsley, or crimson dwarf nasturtiums. Emphasize the bright colors of spring flowers with the green, crinkled leaves of Bloomsdale spinach, and later plant a ground cover of spreading New Zealand spinach. Train Malabar spinach on a fence or trellis behind your flower bed and use its leaves in your summer salads. Fringed, plumelike mustard greens and dark blue dwarf kale, Green Curled endive, and the delicate leaves of Oak Leaf lettuce offer unusual colors and shapes to add to your early and late flower beds.

Later in the season, use the semishade of your tall annuals to tuck in heat-resistant varieties of looseleaf lettuce. Grow some feathery fennel among your annuals; make a backdrop of Chinese cabbage for your low-growing annuals. I once saw Purple Plum petunias intermixed with Green Ice lettuce in a friend's garden. And don't overlook the areas alongside the foundation of your house or the semishaded spots in your landscape where your salad plants will be protected from the summer sun.

Ground is precious, and there isn't any rule that says your yard is for grass only. Think salad circles instead. Dig up the grass (it can always be planted again) and make a circle of plants for your salad bowl. If your soil is hard and clayey, dig some sand and humus into it. Dig in some fertilizer, following the

directions on the package on the amount to use. Plant Ruby or Prizehead lettuce in the middle of such a circle and surround it with another circle of Buttercrunch lettuce and still another with light green Tom Thumb. Make a final circular edging with a dwarf parsley or cress. For the best effect and for the most efficient use of a salad circle, timing is important. Start the plants that take the longest time to mature first. Or start the plants ahead of time in flats or pots and transplant them into the circle when they are all beyond the seedling stage.

Try a circle with a mixture of flowers and salad plants. Plant red-orange Fireglow marigolds in the center, surround them with a looseleaf lettuce, and make a border of dwarf, mixed-color nasturtiums. You can harvest the nasturtiums and lettuce for salads and dry the marigold flowers to use in place of saffron.

You can go round and round (sorry) with combinations of colors, textures, and tastes in salad circles as long as you keep in mind the growing requirements of the plants during the different times of the season.

PATIOS, PORCHES, BALCONIES, TERRACES

If ground space is too limited or if you are a city dweller or a mobile home owner, you can become a container farmer.

Containers come in all sizes, shapes, and materials, both decorative and plain. I find the best are the porous wood and clay ones. Plastic and aluminum will do if you punch holes in their sides at their bottoms. Good drainage is very important — never let any container sit in water. Provide brick or wooden frames or saucers filled with small stones to catch water overflow. Whichever size and type of container you choose, make sure that it is at least 8 inches deep.

Growing plants in containers, particularly leafy vegetables, involves extra vigilance; you must make sure the soil does not dry out and you have to protect the plants from hot sun. One of the advantages of container farming is that you can move the containers into the shade during the hottest time of the day. Large containers can be mounted on wheels and rolled around.

Apartment dwellers should be realistic about trying to grow tender greens during the summer months when wind, heat, and glare could make doing so a frustrating and useless project. Best to harvest leafy greens before the hot days arrive and plant them again in early August for a fall crop. The time between can be used for heat-loving vegetables such as tomatoes, peppers, eggplants, and cucumbers. Now that I have said all this, I may have to take it back. A young friend who is an enthusiastic New York City terrace farmer has told me that he grew leaf lettuce all last summer on his terrace, which gets sun nearly all day. When I asked him how in the world he could do this, he told me he grew his lettuce in a window box that had good drainage and that he nearly drowned it every morning. His lettuce came up "like crazy" and he had no problems with it at all. So there you are.

Soil for Containers

If garden soil is available, by all means use it. So the soil will hold water and not pack down, use the following mix:

1 part garden soil
1 part finished compost or peat moss
1 part vermiculite or sand

(Peat moss is acid. If you use it, add some crushed limestone or dolomite to the mix — 1 tablespoon to 3 quarts of mix.)

If no garden soil is handy, buy packaged sterile soil. Add to it as you would to garden soil.

Lighter and easier to handle are the Cornell peat mixes, or "soil-less soils," which go under the commercial names of Jiffy Mix, Pro-Mix, and Kys-Mix. I have found that they have one disadvantage: after some use they tend to pack down and lose their air- and water-holding capacities, causing plants to become spindly and weak. To remedy this, add ½ part vermiculite or sand to 1 part mix. This gives you a growing medium that can be used over and over again with fertilizer added on a regular schedule. (See below.) Stir up the medium each time you use it. The Cornell scientists have also come out with a plastic container filled with their peat-lite mix, called Pillow Paks. All you need to do is

to plant your seeds or seedlings in the slits cut into the top of the pillow, which you can then set in a window box or other container or directly on the patio or terrace.

When you water these light mixes, water them from the bottom or use a very fine spray on their surfaces to prevent erosion. Regular watering of your container farm, no matter what kind of soil you use, is essential.

Mulching Containers

To keep garden and sterile soil mixes from drying out fast in hot weather, mulch the soil, once the plants are well up, with pebbles, coarse gravel, grass clippings, shredded newspaper, black plastic, etc. For a more elegant effect, use a bark mulch. Mulch "soil-less soils" with inorganic material such as pebbles, coarse gravel, or black plastic to keep them sterile.

FERTILIZING CONTAINER FARMS

Because they are simple to use and give my crops all the nutrients they need, I use liquid seaweed and liquid fish emulsion, varying the two to give my crops a change of diet. When I seed my containers, I water them with liquid seaweed. Then, once the plants are up, I fertilize them every other week using liquid seaweed one time and liquid fish emulsion the next.

Good, too, are blood meal, bone meal, and the vegetable meals. If you use these dry fertilizers, mix them into the soil when you are preparing it, following the directions on the packages for the amounts to use. As you don't have to worry about any chemical buildup in the soil, you can use these dry organic fertilizers year round in your container farm — as you can liquid seaweed and fish emulsion.

WHAT TO GROW

Lettuce and other salad greens, fruiting salad vegetables, some root vegetables, and herbs can all be grown in containers with great success. (See the next chapter for a specific list of salad crops I recommend growing indoors. These are as good, or better, for outdoors containers.) Lettuce and other leafy greens should be harvested before they are mature, as they will not have the room to reach maturity unless enough space is provided — at least 6 to 7 inches for each plant. If you want a mature head of lettuce, grow it separately in a 6-inch pot. A round ceramic pot with a Great Lakes head lettuce in it makes a handsome addition to any patio, porch, or terrace. So does a tub with a couple of cherry tomato plants surrounded by leaf lettuce. I don't see anything wrong either with large wooden boxes filled with lettuce or spinach or a combination of greens. Beautiful!

VERTICAL GARDENS

Think vertically for a real space-saving salad garden. Odd or unusual as it may seem, leafy greens and fruiting salad vegetables can be grown in upright fashions in hanging wire cylinders or tall free-standing boxes on wheels and dividers. There are many plans and ways of making these gardens. You can use cheap materials like fine-meshed chicken wire to make a small hanging vertical garden or you can use expensive redwood to make vertical boxes and solid fences that act as dividers for privacy or for aesthetic reasons.

One summer I built a small hanging wire cylinder garden for my lettuce to see how it would work. It worked very well and it was simple to make. I nailed two 4-foot wooden slats to a circular board 8 inches in diameter and attached fine-meshed chicken wire around the slats. I then lined the column with black plastic, filled it with Jiffy Mix, and watered it with liquid seaweed. Next, I poked holes through the wire mesh, 4 inches apart, and planted Ruby and Salad Bowl lettuce plants in the holes, slanting them upward and staggering the varieties for the color effect. Finally, I attached picture wire to the planter and hung the whole affair on my porch, where it got six hours of sun a day. (I had to turn the planter every other day, as I didn't use the fisherman's swivel as advised in the directions.) By the time the lettuce was mature enough to harvest, it had covered the black plastic and looked so pretty I hated to pick it. But I did, and the lettuce kept flourishing as long as I kept picking the outside leaves, kept the soil moist, and fed the plants every other week.

Besides saving space, hanging vertical gardens are light enough so that you can move them into the shade if the weather turns hot. Or it can work the other way around. A hanging vertical garden of herbs, for instance, that you grow indoors can be moved outdoors for a breath of fresh air and sun for several hours a day. Free-standing vertical boxes on wheels can be turned to take advantage of the sun or to avoid too much of it.

Chapter Eight

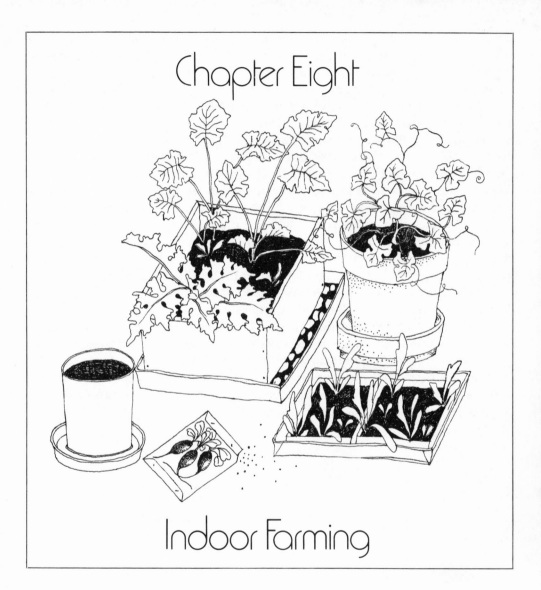

Indoor Farming

I BECAME an indoor farmer quite unintentionally when I was living in New York City. One September, a friend who lived upstate brought me a geranium plant as a house present. I put the plant in a sunny window and it flourished. By and by, I noticed that some other plant, not at all like a geranium, was growing in the pot. It looked suspiciously like a tomato seedling, which indeed it was, a very sturdy little plant that grew rapidly in company with its flowering neighbor.

When I told my friend about the extra bonus she had given me, she said she had dug the earth for the geranium out of her vegetable garden near her cherry tomatoes and what I had was a volunteer plant. She advised me to transplant it into a 6-inch pot, stake it, and when it flowered to pollinate the flowers with a cotton swab or camel's-hair brush with tiny bristles, and gently transfer the pollen from one flower to the other. She told me it was necessary to hand-pollinate tomatoes and peppers grown indoors in order for them to set fruit. I followed her directions except for the transplanting. I simply tied the tomato plant to the geranium and waited to see what would happen. In November, the star attractions in my apartment were the orange-red cherry tomatoes amid the purple-red flowers of the geranium. I have been an indoor farmer ever since.

Whether you grow one tomato plant or just enough lettuce for a few salads, or turn every inch of available space you have into an indoor farm, I guarantee it will be worth your while. Indoor farming can be a boon to apartment dwellers, mobile home owners, shut-ins, and senior citizens who want a hobby that is health-giving as well as fun. What's more, you can farm indoors any time of the year, as you are the one who controls light, moisture, and temperature to suit the needs of your indoor crops.

WHERE TO FARM INDOORS

IN NATURAL LIGHT

Leaf and root vegetables need 6 hours of sunlight a day, fruiting vegetables need 8. If you are fortunate enough to have such glorious light, by all means take advantage of it. (You may have to use supplemental light during the winter. See below.) Be careful, however, of the strength of a hot summer sun and protect your crops with bamboo or light filmy curtains or venetian blinds to filter the light. Window greenhouses are terrific additions for indoor crops. Balcony and terrace owners can grow leafy greens all winter in a simple hotbed. Use a small wooden box (about 14 by 18 inches by at least 8 inches deep) and install an inexpensive heating cable in its bottom. Cover with soil and plant. The box can be covered with heavy plastic nailed to a frame to fit the top of the box. During the severest weather, cover the box with an old blanket. Acrylic bubbles are being used to cover cellar window wells for indoor gardens.

UNDER FLUORESCENT LIGHT

If you do not have enough natural light or need to supplement it, fluorescent light is ideal for growing lettuce and other salad greens. You need only to buy a standard 48-inch tube reflector with one cool white and one warm white 40-watt bulb. (Basic light setups come in shorter and longer lengths. The size or sizes you buy depend on the space you have and how many indoor crops you want to grow. Two 48-inch setups hung side by side are what I use.) These lights are the highest in light intensity of the standard tubes and do not need to be supplemented. There seems to be some disagreement on the type of fluorescents needed for growing fruiting vegetables indoors. Some say you must have the special plant tubes such as Gro-Lux, Plant-Gro, Vita-Life, and Agro-lite to provide the pink and blue spectrums necessary for flowering. Others say the standard cool and warm lights will do just as well. I am in agreement with the latter opinion, although I find the best light for fruiting vegetables is sunlight supplemented by artificial light during the short days of winter. If you want to invest in the special plant tubes, I'm not trying to discourage you from doing so, I am only trying to save you a little money. If you decide on them, your leafy crops will do well under them too.

Lights should be left on 14 hours a day and suspended 4 inches above the seedlings, and moved up as the seedlings grow. If you are only going to grow leafy vegetables you can leave the lights on 24 hours a day. This may sound extravagant but it isn't. Leaving fluorescent lights on all the time will actually cost you less than switching them on and off twice a day.

TEMPERATURE AND HUMIDITY

Leafy vegetables do best at temperatures from 50° to 68° F. and fruiting vegetables, from 60° to 78° F. If your house or apartment is hot and dry, you can help the situation by setting your plants on a watertight tray filled with pebbles. Add water until it reaches just below the top layer of the pebbles. A daily misting helps raise the humidity, too, but I think it is more of a chore than using a pebble tray. You can buy galvanized steel trays, cheaper plastic trays, or you can use aluminum cake and roasting pans. Vegetables growing in clay pots can be set in clay saucers filled with sphagnum moss kept damp. Be sure to set the pot and saucer on a piece of plastic or other waterproof material, as the moisture can cause floor or furniture damage. Other ways of raising the humidity are to set bowls of water among your crops and to place pans of water on the tops of radiators. An automatic humidifier can be as beneficial to you well as to your crops.

SOIL

I've talked about the different soil mixes for container gardening in the last chapter. The only thing I would like to add is that if you use your garden soil indoors, it is best to screen it first and then bake it in a 350° oven for an hour. This sterilizes the soil and gets rid of all the weed seeds and pests lurking in it and also helps prevent damping off — a fungus disease that young seedlings are prone to when grown indoors. It is fatal.

CONTAINERS

Containers for leafy salad vegetables should be at least 8 inches deep. For fruiting salad vegetables, use gallon-size containers. Be innovative and look around your home, local five-and-ten, supermarket, and junk dealer for containers that will serve your purposes and not cost you an arm and a leg. I found a grapefruit crate behind our supermarket which I lined with plastic. I punched holes in the plastic and filled the crate with good garden soil mixed with compost, vermiculite, and a handful of bone meal. (I sterilized the soil-compost mixture first.) I use it over and over again to grow lush, tender lettuce under my light setup in the cellar. Other ideas for containers are old barrel kegs cut in half, window boxes, plastic refrigerator crispers, dishpans, half-gallon milk containers with the top cut off, coffee cans. Hanging baskets do nicely for midget cucumbers, cherry tomatoes, and herbs. Vertical gardens can be used indoors for your salad crops either in natural light or under artificial light.

WATERING

Water leafy vegetables at least once a day and fruiting and root vegetables every other day, but never allow the soil to get soggy in any case. And please don't shock your crops out of a week's growth by dowsing them with cold water. Use lukewarm water. Even better, use water that has been left in an open container for twenty-four hours to get rid of the chlorine. I don't always do this and I've never killed an indoor or an outdoor crop yet.

FERTILIZING

The feeding schedule I advised for your outdoor container crops applies to your indoor ones as well. If you have a blender you can do some indoor "garbage gardening" à la Ruth Stout. Into your blender put your vegetable scraps and leftovers, coffee grounds, eggshells (but no meat), and add enough water to make a liquid. Blend at high speed and serve your crops a real treat every couple of weeks in place of watering.

Except for whitefly, I have not had any other pests on my indoor crops, although red spider, aphids, mealy bugs, and scale can be a problem. Use the garlic-Tabasco spray or make a solution of 1 tablespoon of rubbing alcohol to 1 pint of water. Spray once a week but never when your plants are in full sun. It's also helpful to wash infected plants under a strong spray of water and to keep your crops tidy by removing dead leaves.

There's a new idea for trapping whiteflies which I have tried, and it works. Paint both sides of large squares or strips of heavy cardboard bright yellow (a color that attracts whiteflies), then coat them with a sticky substance such as Tack Trap or Tree Tanglefoot. Hang the traps in and around your crops and shake the infected plants. The whiteflies are attracted to the traps like houseflies to flypaper. Recoat the traps every three weeks.

SALAD CROPS FOR AN INDOOR FARM

For me it's a temptation to become a little overcropped. There are all those sunny windows, the light setups, and the curiosity I have to see just how good an indoor farmer I am. Finally, there is the not-so-small desire to beat the supermarket out of its sky-high prices for salad greens. But realism must start somewhere and I can see that making my house into a plantation could become such an overwhelming project that I'd give the whole thing up and take up bridge. That said, I am now going to tell you about the salad crops I've grown indoors over the past few years and let you take on the burden of the size and variety of your indoor farm.

Lettuce and Other Salad Greens
Leafy crops are the easiest of all the crops to grow indoors. They flourish under fluorescent lights and will do well in a west window without supplemental light during the months of longest light. You can sow a flat or other

container of leaf lettuce and use the thinnings in three weeks. To have a continuous crop of leafy greens, harvest them before they are completely mature and then replace the harvested plants with seedlings.

More specifically, when your first planting of lettuce is three weeks old, start a small sowing in another container. As germinating seeds do not need a lot of light, they can be started in any cool, dim place where they won't be in the way. Once the seedlings are up they should be placed under light right away. Continue to make new sowings every three weeks. As you will be harvesting your leafy crops before they are mature, you can grow them close together, 3 to 4 inches apart. If you want more mature leaf lettuce, transplant the plants into larger containers, or thin them out to 6 to 7 inches apart in the container they were started in. Larger greens can be started in peat pots or Jiffy 7's and transplanted into 6-inch pots.

For the best flavor, keep your lettuce and other salad greens growing fast by feeding them every two weeks with a fertilizer high in nitrogen, such as liquid seaweed.

Varieties I recommend trying:

Looseleaf lettuce: Grand Rapids Forcing, Salad Bowl, Oakleaf, Slobolt (excellent for warmer houses and apartments).

Butterhead lettuce: Buttercrunch, Tom Thumb, Summer Bibb.

Crisphead lettuce: Paris White Romaine.

Other salad greens: endive (Green Curled), spinach (New Zealand and Malabar), mustard (Tendergreen), spinach beet, corn salad, chicory (Rossa de Verona), Chinese cabbage (Michihli).

SOME SALAD EXTRAS

FRUITING SALAD VEGETABLES

Cucumbers, peppers, and tomatoes are all welcome additions to indoor farms, particularly during the winter. I am always very proud of my indoor fruiting crops because they look so pretty and are so productive. They also give

the impression of being the result of a large store of agricultural knowledge. Truth is, they are a snap to grow.

Fruiting vegetables do best in a sunny window, next best in a window that gets 4 hours of direct sun a day plus 4 hours of supplemental lighting. For fertilizer, I have had the best results with liquid fish emulsion. Be careful not to overfeed your fruiting crops — they would respond to your "kindness" by growing so fast they'd forget why you planted them and not bother to put out flowers and fruit.

CUCUMBERS

You can plant cucumbers singly in a hanging basket or in a 10-inch pot or in groups of three or four plants in a 5-gallon container. It is best to fertilize the soil before you plant the seeds and feed the plants when they are 5 to 6 inches high. Train your cucumber vines early, before the fruit sets. You can use a stake encircled with chicken wire and set in the center of the container for a support, or provide a trellis, either homemade or the plastic kind available from seed catalogs and garden centers. Cucumber vines love to climb, so watch out or they will take over all your other plants. To control the vines, do not allow the main vine in the center of the plant to grow any higher than the support you have provided for it. Be ruthless and pinch it off. This allows the lateral vines to develop, which you can then train horizontally or parallel to the main vine on a trellis.

Varieties I recommend trying:

Victory (60 days), Lemon (65 days), Patio Pik (miniature, 55 days), Park's Mimicu (miniature, 50 days). A miniature cucumber in one container can keep good company with parsley and dill — it looks pretty and is also very useful.

PEPPERS

A pepper plant is versatile. It produces both flowers and fruit at the same time. Start each pepper plant in an individual peat pot and eight weeks later transplant it into a gallon-size container. Mature plants should be staked to prevent them from toppling over. Except for hot peppers, you can harvest peppers before they are fully mature. (Don't forget that peppers and tomatoes must be hand-pollinated.)

Varieties I recommend trying:

Burpee's Fordhook (65 days), Hybrid Peter Piper (65 days), Italian Sweet (60 days). Hungarian Wax (65 days) is a hot pepper that changes from canary yellow to bright red when it is ripe.

TOMATOES

Pick your own home-grown tomatoes on a January day and it will either bring back the tomatoes of the summer past or start you dreaming of the ones in the summer to come.

You can buy preplanted tomato kits (other vegetable kits are also available) or you can start seedlings in peat pots and transplant them 4 to 6 weeks later into 6-inch pots. Use larger containers if you want more than one plant to a container. Fertilize your tomato plants when you transplant them and then once a week when the fruit is developing. Be careful not to let the temperature go down below 55° F. at night or over 95° F. during the day, as these extremes will cause the blossoms to drop off the plants before they set fruit. Except for tomato plants growing in hanging baskets, tomatoes should be staked. Put a stake in the pot or container at the time you transplant them.

Varieties I recommend trying:

Tiny Tim Red and Tiny Tim Yellow (55 days), Hybrid Patio (70 days), Yellow Pear (70 days), Stokes Vendor (90 days).

ROOT CROPS

Beets, carrots, onions, and radishes are also worth an indoor farmer's while. They are practically foolproof and grow well and fast in a "soil-less soil" mix and under lights. As with leafy vegetables, planning ahead with succession plantings will give you a continuous harvest.

BEETS

This totally edible root vegetable takes a good 50 days to mature and needs a container at least 12 inches deep. Plant seeds sparingly and when they are 2 inches high, thin them to 2½ inches apart. For the best flavor, harvest beets when they are small, about 1½ inches in diameter, and pick every other one.

Varieties I recommend trying:

Early Red Ball (60 days), Burpee's Golden (55 days), Little Egypt (56 days), Tokyo Cross (50 days).

CARROTS

Make sure you match the depth of the container with the variety of carrot grown. Plant the seed directly in the container and thin the seedlings to 3 inches apart when they are six weeks old, when you can pull them as delicious thinnings. Fertilize the remaining carrots and leave them to mature.

Varieties I recommend trying:

Short 'n' Sweet (68 days), Tiny Sweet (60 days), Baby Finger Nantes (65 days).

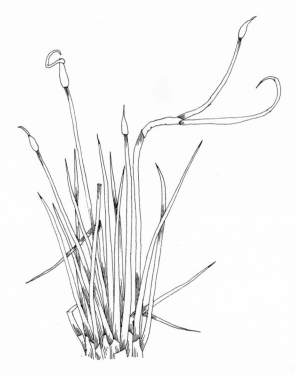

Egyptian Onion

ONIONS

Plant white onion sets (don't bother with onion seed, it will be four months before you can harvest onions started from seed) in containers 8 to 10 inches deep, and fertilize lightly. In five weeks you can harvest scallions that will remind you of spring. Use the tops chopped in salads and when harvesting the whole plant, pull every other one to allow the remaining onions to grow larger bulbs.

For the fun of it as well as the taste, plant one Egyptian onion bulb in an 8-inch container and let it grow to maturity. Give it plenty of water and in 5 to 6 weeks you will have a plant that looks like a giant insect related to a praying mantis.

There are so many kinds of radishes that I suggest you consult your seed catalogs for the shorter varieties that mature in about three weeks. Fertilize the soil before you plant the seeds and thin the seedlings to 1 inch apart in the container. When you pull up a mature radish, pop in another seed to replace it. Radish plants need lots of water.

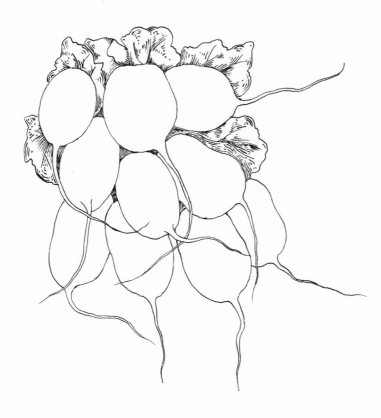

Radishes

I've already gone on at some length about how to grow herbs and other salad enhancements outdoors. Here is how to grow them indoors.

Your herbs will need at least 6 hours of good strong sunlight (turn the pots frequently) or 12 to 14 hours of artificial light. Soil for herbs grown in containers should be good and rich, as the plants use up the nutrients in the soil quickly. Use garden soil, sterilized soil, or a "soil-less soil" mix and fertilize your herbs once a month. The temperature should range from 70° F. by day to 60° F. at night. Herbs don't like drafts — during cold weather it is a good idea to stretch pieces of plastic across your windows to protect your plants. When watering herbs, water them from the top when the soil is dry to the touch but don't let your plants stand in water, which will get stagnant and rot their roots. If you bring herb plants in from your garden, choose the small plants; they will grow better indoors than the larger ones. Try to keep your herbs bushy by snipping off the tops to keep them from flowering. You will find that your herbs do not flourish from November through January, preferring to rest during these months. Keep snipping their tops anyway and they will reward your efforts by sending out new green shoots by the end of January. The best time to start herbs from seed is in the fall for a winter harvest. Pots for single herbs should be 4 to 6 inches across; spreading herbs need containers 8 to 9 inches deep.

Basil, Sweet Green

Sow 2 to 3 seeds in a pot and thin to leave the sturdiest plant to mature. Keep picking the leaves and, if you like basil, start another plant when the first one is three weeks old.

Basil, Purple

Keep one plant to a 6-inch pot. When mature, it makes a very handsome houseplant. Its dark purple leaves are an attractive garnish for leaf lettuce salads.

Chervil germinates quickly and grows fast, so make several sowings after the initial one.

CHIVES

Buy a plant and put it in a 6-inch pot. If you are bringing chives in from your garden, cut the plant down, divide it into small plants, and pot them outdoors. If you let your potted chives freeze before you bring them in, it will spur them into new vigorous growth indoors.

CHIVES, GARLIC

Buy several bulbs and grow them in a large container. They will grow 18 to 24 inches high.

CRESS (PEPPERGRASS)

Grown indoors, cress can be harvested in two weeks. Sow it on a damp sponge set in a saucer and put it in a sunny window or under lights. Keep the sponge damp. Three or four thicknesses of a blotter will also work. Or even a doormat kept damp and set in a sunny place. I like to grow cress with a cherry tomato plant — the bright green bushy foliage looks very pretty and also serves to cover up the base of the tomato plant, which can get straggly looking. Try planting a pot with both cress and mustard seeds for a real spicy mixture to flavor your salads with. If you love cress, make successive sowings every two weeks.

DILL

Easy to grow from seed, dill will grow quickly indoors. Allow several plants to grow in a 5-inch pot and keep reseeding, as a dill plant has a short life.

GARLIC

Six bulbs in an 8-inch pot will give you plenty of garlic greens. Maybe too many.

MARJORAM, SWEET

Easy to grow from seed, marjoram does well indoors. It likes to be kept warm and it hates wet feet.

PARSLEY

If you bring in parsley plants from outdoors, be sure they are new growth. Because it has a long taproot, parsley needs a deep pot. If you grow parsley from seed, soak the seeds in water for 24 hours, then plant the seeds and keep the pot in shade until the seedlings appear. Parsley likes to be kept cool and does well under lights. Fertilize it very lightly during the winter months and use the outside leaves to keep the plants vigorous.

ROCKET

Grown indoors, rocket stays small, about 6 inches high. Plant it fairly thickly and keep cutting it back for new growth.

SALAD BURNET

If you bring salad burnet in from your garden, select young plants and put them in a 5 by 7-inch flat or other shallow container. (Five plants should be sufficient.) Add some lime and sand to the soil and keep the soil on the dry side. Or start from seed and transplant into a larger container in about three weeks.

TARRAGON

Pot up tarragon in an 8- to 10-inch pot and keep the soil dry to the touch, but don't let it dry out completely. When cutting, leave 2 inches of stem for future growth.

THYME

It is best to buy thyme plants for indoor growing. Keep the plants bushy by snipping their tops and don't water them too much.

The best place to grow watercress is in a northwest window (never in full sun) in moist sphagnum moss set in a shallow container. Sift potting soil over the moss to cover it to 2 inches from the top of the container. Sprinkle watercress seeds on top of the soil and cover them with a thin layer of shredded moss. Now add water to the top of the container. The plants grow from 6 to 8 inches high. For a continuous supply of watercress, keep reseeding with sprouted seeds. Sprout watercress seeds as you do lettuce seeds: soak seeds in a half-cup of water for two days or sprinkle them on a wet paper towel; enclose them in a plastic bag, tie it shut, and leave it in a dim place for two days.

FLOWERS

CALENDULA

Calendulas do very well indoors in full sun. They need 6-inch pots for each plant. You can bring in small plants from your garden or start seedlings in a flat or peat pots and transplant them into pots. They will brighten your indoor farm all winter if you pick the flowers regularly.

NASTURTIUM

By all means include nasturtiums in your indoor farm. They will do well both in full sun or in a north window. To get nasturtiums going, soak the seeds overnight, then plant them in small pots or window boxes and keep them shaded until the seedlings appear. Aphids love nasturtiums, so keep after the aphids by spraying them weekly with soap and water, or use a mixture of 1 part water and 1 part milk.

VIOLETS

Bring in a clump of the smallest plants from your garden and pot them up in 6-inch pots or window boxes in the soil in which they grew. Put them in a sunny window; keep picking the flowers and they will bloom all winter.

SPROUTED SEEDS

Sprouted seeds are such vitamin-filled additions to salads (and other foods) that I feel I would be letting you down if I didn't add them to the indoor farm's salad crops. Buy seeds, from health food stores, such as alfalfa (my favorite), mung beans, soy beans, pinto beans, wheat, lentils, sunflower, etc. Soak a small amount of seeds overnight in a wide-mouth glass jar covered with a double layer of cheesecloth or nylon stocking secured with a rubber band. In the morning, pour the water out of the jar and rinse the seeds with clean water and drain well. Three times a day, rinse and drain well. Sprouts will be ready in three or four days. If you want to turn your sprouts green, line a shallow pan with several layers of damp paper towels. Spread the sprouts on the paper towels and put the pan under lights or in indirect sun for a day or two. Mist once a day.

Chapter Nine

Outdoor Lettuce—
Nine to Twelve Months a Year

I T WAS a cold night in late fall and I was having a dinner party. When I brought in the salad bowl a guest remarked that the lettuce looked like fresh garden lettuce. "It is," I said. "In fact, I picked it this afternoon."

In this chapter, which is for ambitious backyard gardeners, I will explain how you, too, can impress your friends and please your family and yourself by growing lettuce outdoors all year, or nearly all year. I have to add "nearly" for gardeners who live in areas where the winters are long and severe (zones 1–3). They should omit the months of December, January, and February and use the program to grow lettuce in the coldframe in early spring and late fall. There are exceptions to this rule, though. I live in zone 3, but our area is in a warm pocket of the zone, so I am able to grow lettuce in my coldframe without any man-made heat until December. After December, without adding any heat, my lettuce plants do not grow but "winter over" and begin growing again in late February to give me nice large lettuce in April and May. However, by converting my coldframe into a simple hotbed, I can grow several plantings of lettuce right through the winter months.

The basic idea of this program is to grow a continual supply of lettuce in your garden during the regular season, and then to grow it as long as possible in a coldframe during the off-growing season. This latter requires starting your seedlings indoors to grow replacements for the plants you harvest in the coldframe. You might ask, why bother to grow lettuce outdoors during the off-growing season at all when you can grow it indoors on a windowsill or under lights? My answer is, because you can grow larger, crisper lettuce, even head lettuce, which doesn't do well indoors. Also, I enjoy the challenge and I think it's fun. I admit there's some trial and error involved and you have to invest in some special equipment, but there are weekends when you might not have much to do and you'll be glad you're growing lettuce outdoors. (Perhaps you'll enjoy doing it so much you'll grow other salad greens as well.)

THE COLDFRAME

A coldframe is not a poor man's greenhouse. It is unique unto itself, serving purposes that a greenhouse does not. Basically, a coldframe is a bottomless box,

covered by glass or plastic, which sits on the ground and is heated by the sun.
When you add man-made heat to a coldframe it becomes a hotbed.

You can use a coldframe for many purposes: to propagate seeds and cuttings, harden off vegetables and flowers before planting them in the garden, carry cuttings through the winter, store root vegetables, stretch your vegetable crops, experiment with new plants, make compost, and grow lettuce off-season. There are various kinds and sizes of coldframes and many ways to build them. You can buy aluminum frames, with tops that automatically open and close, for around fifty dollars, or you can build a frame out of cement blocks or wood.

The coldframe I use, which my husband made at very little cost, is made of boards to fit an old storm window 2½ by 5 feet. The back of the frame is 18 inches high and the front is 9 inches. The tilt is to get the maximum amount of sun and to let the rain run off the glass. The back of the storm window is hinged with door hinges to the back of the frame. If you don't have a storm window you can use a window screen and cover it with heavy plastic, using staples to fasten the plastic down. Be sure you fasten the screen to the front of the frame with a hook and eye to keep it from blowing open.

In freezing weather, you will need material to cover the coldframe. You can use old blankets, a tarpaulin, a sheet of heavy plastic, or two pieces of burlap stuffed with straw and stitched up the sides.

In hot weather I use a double thickness of cheesecloth draped over the open frame. Or you can make a lathe shade. The shade is necessary to protect the seedlings when you make your first planting in September when the weather can be hot.

An outdoor extension cord and a 60-watt bulb will make the coldframe into a simple hotbed.

LOCATION
Set the coldframe, facing south, in a protected sunny spot as close to your house and to a water outlet as possible to save you steps.

SOIL
The soil should be good and rich in the coldframe. Use 2 parts good garden soil and 1 part sand. If you are setting your coldframe on sod, it is best to turn

the sod over before putting the soil on top of it to get a good, deep seed bed and so the grass won't come poking up through the soil. Add at least 8 inches of soil and then mix in a handful of organic fertilizer. Water the soil well and let it sit for a week. Just before planting time, stir the soil and remove any large stones and weeds. Then firm the soil down and rake it until it is smooth, and water it again.

SEED-STARTING MEDIUM

For the best results in starting your seedlings indoors to be transplanted into the coldframe, I advise using special mediums such as square 2¼-inch peat pots filled with a soil-less soil, compressed peat pellets, or 1-inch specially prepared Fertl Cubes. These are easy to use and, more important, there is less shock to the seedlings when they are transplanted. You will also need a tray filled with vermiculite to set the pots or pellets in to provide good drainage and humidity for the seedlings.

You are now ready for the month-by-month program. The program is written for general weather conditions around New York City (zone 3). Gardeners in other areas of the country will have to adjust the timetable to suit the climatic conditions of their zones. And please take into account that no matter where you live, the weather is able to throw the best-laid lettuce plans off their schedules.

SEPTEMBER

By the first of September, have your coldframe ready to go and be sure the soil in it is moist but not soggy. To see how the different kinds of lettuce will grow under the specific weather conditions in your area, I suggest you plant three kinds of lettuce: crisphead, butterhead, and looseleaf. For a head start, sprout your seeds before planting them. Plant the seeds, 4 to 6 seeds to a group, with 6 to 8 inches between the groups. When the seedlings are 1½ inches high or have 4 leaves, thin out the weakest ones, leaving the strongest plant in each group. You can use the thinnings to transplant into spaces where seeds have not come up properly or have met with slugs. Slugs like the warmth of cold-frames, so be on the alert for them. After you have thinned your seedlings, you should now have approximately 36 plants in your coldframe. Be sure to keep the ground moist and to shade the open frame if the weather gets hot.

At the end of September, indoors, start the seedlings that will replace the plants you will harvest from the coldframe. Sow 2 to 3 seeds to each peat pot or cube and put them in a tray filled with vermiculite far enough apart so that the moist vermiculite surrounds each pot or cube. The number of pots or cubes that you seed depends on the rate at which your lettuce grows in the coldframe and the amount of lettuce you use. I would advise starting with 16 pots or cubes. Place the tray in a cool place where it does not get direct light. As soon as the seeds germinate, put the tray in a sunny window or under lights. If you use lights, suspend or set them 4 inches above the seedlings, moving them up as the seedlings grow, and leave the lights on 24 hours a day. When the seedlings are 1½ inches high, thin them by snipping them off with scissors at their base, leaving the strongest seedling to each pot or cube. Keep the seedlings moist, and every other week feed them with a liquid fertilizer. Mist them frequently.

OCTOBER

Watch for sudden drops in temperature, when you should close the cold-frame three hours before sunset and cover the frame at night. By the middle to the end of October, you can start harvesting the lettuce in the coldframe and re-placing it with the seedlings grown indoors. To lessen the shock of the cold out-doors, cut down by half the water you give your seedlings for one week before you transplant them. The day you transplant, water them well with a liquid fertilizer. Bring any leftover seedlings back into the house and put them in a sunny window or under lights again. You can pot them up to grow larger replacements for your plants in the coldframe. At the end of October, or begin-ning of November, sow a new batch of pots or cubes. Now is a good time to try three different varieties of the hardiest lettuces. Again, the amount you plant depends on how many plants you need to replace the plants in the coldframe.

Continue to harvest and replace the plants in the coldframe. At the end of November, or the beginning of December, start another batch of seedlings.

SPECIAL PRECAUTIONS FOR SEVERE COLD

1. Be sure to close the coldframe three to four hours before sunset and cover it at night with a blanket or other protective material.
2. Hill up around the coldframe's outside edges with dirt, hay, or leaves.
3. Water the soil in the coldframe in the morning only.
4. Mulch the plants.
5. Keep the coldframe closed during the day. If you see moisture collecting on the glass or plastic, it means a lack of ventilation and you should open the top anywhere from 1 inch to 2 feet, depending on the temperature and the amount of wind.
6. Line the inside boards of the coldframe with aluminum foil to amplify and reflect the light and heat.
7. Rig up an outdoor extension wire and 60-watt bulb. Run the wire under the coldframe and place the bulb in the middle of the coldframe on a piece of aluminum foil. You now have a temporary hotbed which will keep your lettuce from freezing. With this simple device, my lettuce has stayed as perky and as healthy as you please. If your lettuce plants should suffer from a freeze before you install the light bulb, sprinkle them with water and they will revive. There are other ways you can convert your coldframe into a simple, temporary hotbed. I have never tried them so I can't vouch for them, but here they are anyway: put bowls of boiling water in the coldframe at night; line the insides of the coldframe with manure; or put warm bags of hay on top of the coldframe at night before covering it.
8. During and after snowfalls, leave the snow on the coldframe — snow is an excellent insulator and, unless the snow is a foot thick (in which case you should brush it off), enough light will filter through it to keep the lettuce healthy. Wait until the weather warms up a little before you open the frame.

9. I am sure you won't go out in the freezing weather to do your transplanting, but will wait for a break in the weather. When you get a nice, sunny day, transplant your seedlings quickly, water and mulch them, and give them some air. They'll love you for it.

DECEMBER–JANUARY–FEBRUARY

Carry on the schedule of harvesting and reseeding every three to four weeks. Your schedule will depend on how fast the plants are growing during these cold months and at what stage of their growth you harvest the lettuce in the coldframe.

MARCH

End of February, first of March, seed your pots or cubes for the final time for transplanting into the coldframe. Mid-March, transplant all your seedlings into the coldframe and sow lettuce seeds directly in the ground in your garden, weather conditions permitting (or when the ground is workable). At the end of March, make another planting of lettuce in your garden and into flats also if you wish to have "standby lettuce" for transplanting into the garden. Watch for cold spells and keep the coldframe protected.

APRIL

Harvest lettuce as it matures from the coldframe. Keep making successive plantings in the garden (or in flats) every two to three weeks. Middle to end of April, harvest lettuce thinnings from the garden. Leave the coldframe uncovered unless there is a freeze.

MAY–JUNE

By now, if all has gone well, you will have harvested all your lettuce from the coldframe and are harvesting lettuce from the garden. In June, make plantings of hot-weather varieties in the garden (or in flats). Thin and harvest the plants as they mature. Keep the plants mulched.

JULY–AUGUST

Shade lettuce plants in the garden with a cheesecloth tent or lattice. Keep making successive plantings of hot-weather varieties, using the techniques to speed germination in hot weather described in Chapter Two. A mid-August planting of cool-weather varieties will carry you over until the first hard frost. At the end of August, prepare your coldframe to seed it the first of September. If you have any leftover seedlings or immature plants, transplant them into the coldframe before the first frost to get a jump on the year-round program.

Chapter Ten

Recipes

First, a few salad making do's and don'ts. Don't ever, ever drown your salad in dressing. The object is to coat the leaves of the greens with the dressing, not get them soaking wet and soggy. One-fourth to one-half cup of dressing is plenty to add to a salad for four. If you are adding the separate ingredients of the dressing at the table, do add the oil first so as to coat the leaves and give the other seasonings something to cling to. Do, always, wash, dry, and crisp your greens before you use them. Don't toss your salad when you are mad at someone or feeling cross generally. Salads should be thoroughly but *lightly* tossed.

A good rule for dressing the different kinds of lettuce is to add the salad dressing to butterhead and looseleaf lettuces just before serving — this applies to mixed greens also — and to dress crisphead lettuces 15 minutes before serving.

For the basic ingredients of a dressing, I recommend olive oil or peanut oil. Good, too, is a mixture of half olive oil and half sesame oil.

For vinegar, I prefer red wine and my own herb vinegars.

Black pepper is best when it is freshly ground. And try the coarsely ground or some of the seasoned salts for a change from regular salt. A seasoned salt can sometimes pep up a salad dressing that has turned out too bland and it can add new tastes to a basic French dressing.

BASIC FRENCH DRESSING
1 cup olive oil or salad oil
¼ cup wine vinegar
1 teaspoon salt
½ teaspoon freshly ground black pepper
½ teaspoon dry mustard

Place all the ingredients in a bottle with a top, or a screw-top jar, and shake vigorously. Store at room temperature and use within 4 to 5 days.

Variations: You can vary Basic French Dressing by adding such ingredients as chopped chives, garlic, capers, chutney, horseradish, Roquefort cheese, an- chovies, etc. Lemon juice may be substituted for the vinegar. You may also use herb, malt, cider, or other vinegars.

BLENDER FRENCH DRESSING
¼ cup vinegar (herb or red or white wine)
¾ cup olive oil or salad oil
¼ teaspoon dry mustard
1 tablespoon lemon juice
Salt and freshly ground black pepper to taste
Put all the ingredients into a blender and blend at high speed for 20 seconds.

VINAIGRETTE DRESSING
To 1 cup Basic French Dressing add: chopped green olives, capers, parsley, chives, chopped sweet pickles, finely chopped hard-cooked egg, Dijon mustard.

HERB FRENCH DRESSING
¾ cup olive oil or salad oil
¼ cup tarragon vinegar
¾ teaspoon salt
¼ teaspoon freshly ground black pepper
1 teaspoon chopped fresh basil
Place all the ingredients in a bottle with a top or a screw-top jar and shake vigorously. Store at room temperature and use within 4 to 5 days.

CHIFFONADE DRESSING
Combine ½ cup Basic French Dressing with 2 tablespoons very finely minced green pepper, 2 tablespoons diced pimiento, 1 hard-cooked egg chopped fine. Chill.

LEMON BALM DRESSING

¾ cup olive oil or salad oil
¼ cup lemon juice
1 teaspoon salt
¼ teaspoon freshly ground black pepper
1 teaspoon finely chopped parsley
1 teaspoon finely chopped lemon balm leaves
1 teaspoon finely chopped chives
½ teaspoon prepared mustard

Mix all the ingredients together with a cube of ice until mixture thickens slightly. Remove ice and chill. Good for tossed greens and Chinese cabbage coleslaw.

SPRING SCALLION DRESSING

1 cup sour cream (or yogurt if you are dieting)
2½ cups mayonnaise (or "diet" mayonnaise)
2 teaspoons lemon juice
1 cup thinly chopped scallions with tops
¼ teaspoon salt

Beat the sour cream and mayonnaise together. Add the lemon juice, scallions, and salt. Chill.

TANGY DRESSING

1 teaspoon chili powder
2 cups salad oil
1 teaspoon salt
1 teaspoon garlic powder
¼ cup tomato catsup
¼ cup old-fashioned dark molasses
¾ cup cider vinegar

Combine the first four ingredients; let them stand 1 hour. Add the rest of the ingredients and beat thoroughly with an eggbeater.

BACON DRESSING

2 pieces of bacon, diced
¾ cup Basic French Dressing
2 hard-cooked eggs, chopped fine
Dash of sugar
Salt to taste

Cook the bacon until crisp and drain it on a paper towel. Combine the bacon with the rest of the ingredients and mix well. Add more salt to the dressing if needed. (A seasoned salt gives this dressing a tangy taste.) Good for spinach and other greens.

CHIVE DRESSING

6 anchovy fillets, chopped
1 scallion, chopped fine
½ cup finely chopped fresh chives
¼ cup fresh parsley, minced
1 tablespoon dried tarragon or 2 tablespoons fresh, chopped
⅛ teaspoon garlic powder
¼ cup wine vinegar
3 cups mayonnaise

Mix the anchovies and scallion together. Put them into a bowl and add the chives, parsley, tarragon, and garlic powder. Stir in the vinegar and mayonnaise and mix well. Let stand 1 hour before using. Good with a mixed green salad.

MUSTARD DRESSING

Mix together 1 teaspoon prepared mustard, a little salt, a little freshly ground black pepper, ½ teaspoon lemon juice, and ½ cup of heavy cream.

HEARTS OF LETTUCE OR ROMAINE DRESSING

1 3-ounce package cream cheese, softened
1 cup Basic French Dressing
½ cup chili or tomato sauce
½ cup mayonnaise
Salt and freshly ground black pepper to taste

Whip the cream cheese with the French dressing. Add the other ingredients and stir well. Chill. Pour over hearts of lettuce or romaine and garnish with cranberry jelly.

CREAMY DRESSING

6 tablespoons heavy cream
2 tablespoons lemon juice
⅛ teaspoon Dijon mustard
Salt and freshly ground black pepper to taste

Mix the ingredients together and serve over chicory greens, endive, or celery.

DRESSING FOR COLESLAWS AND GREENS

2 eggs, well beaten
1 tablespoon sugar
1 tablespoon butter
½ tablespoon dry mustard
¼ cup white vinegar
½ cup heavy cream

Combine the ingredients and heat in a double boiler. Cool. Pour over cabbage. Use hot to pour over such greens as dandelion, spinach, kale, beet tops.

To 1 cup mayonnaise, add ¼ cup chili sauce, 1 chopped hard-cooked egg, 1 tablespoon sweet relish.

LOW CALORIE DRESSING

1 cup plain yogurt
¼ cup tomato, Clamato, or V-8 juice
¼ teaspoon prepared mustard
Dash of Worcestershire sauce
Herbs of your choice
Salt and freshly ground black pepper to taste
Combine all the ingredients and chill.

OIL-LESS DRESSING

To 1 package dry salad dressing mix add ¼ cup malt vinegar and 1 cup water.

HERB VINEGARS

When your herbs are full grown and ready to harvest you can make your own herb vinegars — a pleasant task which is also a rewarding one. Home-made herb vinegars are far superior to commercial brands. To start, I advise making four basic vinegars — tarragon, dill, basil, and garlic, then branch out to others such as salad burnet, lemon balm, fennel, thyme, and marjoram. Or try a mixed herb vinegar with marjoram, tarragon, chives, and summer savory. Then go on and experiment with others.

The best time to pick your herbs is in the early morning just after the dew has dried. Gather just as many as you need and use them quickly, before they lose their aroma. Flowering herbs should be picked before the plants are in full bloom.

Use your herb vinegars in place of wine and cider vinegars to vary your salad dressings in ways that please your taste buds the most. You might make some taste mistakes — it's more likely, however, that you'll come up with some taste triumphs.

USING LEFTOVER WINE

Don't throw out your leftover wine. Mix equal quantities of leftover red wine and cider vinegar or white wine and white vinegar. Bottle and cork it and let it sit for 2 to 3 weeks. You will have a very fine wine vinegar to use in your salad dressings or to use to make herb vinegar by the following methods.

QUICK METHOD — 1 TO 2 WEEKS

2 cups herb leaves, washed and dried
1 cup red or white wine vinegar

— bruise on bottom of bottle w. wooden spoon

Pack the herb leaves loosely in a glass jar or bottle. Heat the vinegar in an enamel or stainless steel pan (vinegar corrodes aluminum) until it is hot but not boiling. Pour the wine vinegar over the herb leaves, leaving 2 inches of space at the top of the container. Close the jar or cork the bottle tightly. Shake the mixture once a day for a week, then taste the vinegar for flavor. If it is not strong enough, leave it for another week, shaking the mixture each day. When the vinegar is well flavored, strain it through a fine plastic strainer or cheesecloth and bottle it. For looks, you can add a sprig of the herb to the bottle.

LONGER METHOD — 3 WEEKS TO A MONTH

2 cups herb leaves
1 quart red or white wine vinegar

Put the herb leaves into a crock or glass or china bowl. Pour on cold vinegar and stir and mash the leaves with a wooden spoon. Cover the container. Every other day, stir and crush the leaves. Always cover the container. The vinegar should be ready in three weeks to one month. Strain and bottle as described above.

GARLIC WINE VINEGAR

Put 4 to 6 peeled garlic cloves into 2 cups red wine vinegar. Let it stand for 24 hours. Remove the garlic.

MIXED GREEN SALAD
Combine Bibb lettuce, watercress, curly endive, spinach leaves, and chives, the amount depending on how many you are serving. Dress the salad with Basic French Dressing to which has been added a mashed clove of garlic.

MIXED GREENS WITH ONION AND ORANGES
1 quart mixed greens
2 navel oranges
1 cup thinly sliced red onion rings
¼ cup Basic French Dressing made with lemon juice instead of vinegar
Tear the greens into small pieces and put into a salad bowl with the orange slices. Scatter the onion rings on top, add the dressing, and toss lightly. Serves 4.

TOSSED GREEN SALAD
½ head crisphead lettuce
¼ head curly endive
1 head butterhead lettuce
12 spinach beet leaves
Peppergrass leaves to taste
½ cucumber, thinly sliced
½ bunch red radishes, thinly sliced
Combine all the ingredients in a salad bowl and toss lightly with Spring Scallion Dressing. Serves 6.

BELGIAN ENDIVE SALAD WITH RED CAVIAR

3 large heads Belgian endive
½ cup mayonnaise
½ bunch watercress or upland cress
¼ cup sour cream
1 one-ounce jar red caviar
4 teaspoons catsup
¼ teaspoon onion juice
1 teaspoon lemon juice
Salt and freshly ground black pepper to taste

Cut the endive into halves, lengthwise, and place them on a bed of watercress in a salad bowl. Combine the remaining ingredients and serve over the endive. Serves 4 to 6.

BIBB LETTUCE SALAD

2 to 3 heads Bibb lettuce
1 teaspoon Dijon or Düsseldorf mustard
1 tablespoon wine vinegar or lemon juice
3 tablespoons olive oil or peanut oil
Salt and freshly ground black pepper to taste

Tear the lettuce into small pieces. Put the mustard into a salad bowl and add the remaining ingredients, stirring with a whisk. Add the lettuce and toss. Serves 4.

CAESAR SALAD

¾ cup olive oil
2 cloves garlic, crushed
1 cup croutons made from French or Italian bread
3 heads romaine lettuce
Salt and freshly ground black pepper to taste
1 egg, beaten
1 large lemon, halved
1 tablespoon Worcestershire sauce
8 anchovy fillets, chopped
⅓ cup freshly grated Parmesan or Romano cheese

Combine the oil and garlic and let stand several hours or overnight. Remove the garlic and discard. Heat ¼ cup of the oil in a skillet and brown the croutons. Drain and reserve the croutons. Tear up the lettuce leaves into medium-size pieces and place them in a salad bowl. Add the remaining oil, salt, and pepper and toss. Add the egg and toss until well coated. Squeeze the lemon halves over the salad. Add the Worcestershire sauce, anchovies, and cheese. Toss. Add the croutons and toss again. Serves 8.

CURLY ENDIVE SALAD

1 bunch curly endive
¼ cup finely chopped scallion tops
½ cup peeled; diced cucumber
4 red radishes, thinly sliced

Combine all the ingredients and serve with Basic French Dressing. Serves 4.

CELERY SALAD

4 cups chopped celery
4 tablespoons chopped scallions
2 tablespoons finely chopped parsley
1 cup coarsely chopped sweet red pepper
⅓ cup mayonnaise
Salt and freshly ground black pepper to taste

Toss all the ingredients together, chill, and serve on a bed of lettuce. Serves 4.

CELERY SALAD WITH MUSTARD DRESSING

Wash and crisp 2 bunches of celery. Dice the outer stalks and add the hearts. Serve with Mustard Dressing. Serves 4.

CELERY AND FENNEL SALAD

Chop together equal amounts of celery and fennel stalks, sprinkle with watercress, and serve with Basic French Dressing.

CHINESE CABBAGE SALAD

1 head romaine lettuce
1 head Bibb lettuce
2 cups chopped inner leaves of Chinese cabbage
4 water chestnuts, slivered
½ cup fresh sprouts
1 tablespoon soy sauce
½ cup Basic French Dressing

Tear the lettuce into small pieces; combine with the cabbage, water chestnuts, and sprouts. Add the soy sauce to the Basic French Dressing and mix well. Pour over greens and toss lightly. Serves 4.

CHINESE CABBAGE SLAW

3 cups finely chopped Chinese cabbage
1 green pepper, finely chopped
½ cucumber, chopped

Mix all the ingredients together and serve with Coleslaw Dressing. Serves 4.

CORN SALAD SALAD

Toss corn salad leaves with thinly sliced beets and thinly sliced celery hearts and serve with Basic French Dressing and fresh chervil.

Dandelion Salad

To young dandelion leaves, add Bacon Dressing or hot Coleslaw Dressing or Basic French Dressing. Good, too, are dandelion leaves combined with cold, boiled potatoes and crisply cooked Canadian bacon, tossed lightly together with a small amount of Basic French Dressing.

Fennel Salad

1 bunch fennel with leaves
½ head curly endive
1 cup cooked green beans, chilled
½ cup black olives, sliced

Remove the leafy tops of the fennel. Cut the stalks lengthwise into thin strips and coarsely chop them. Break the curly endive into small pieces. Slice the green beans crosswise. Combine these ingredients in a salad bowl and garnish with the black olives and the chopped fennel leaves. Serve with a garlicky French dressing. Serves 4 to 6.

Hearts of Lettuce Salad with Lemon-Lime Dressing

3 to 4 hearts butterhead lettuce
1 heart romaine lettuce
Freshly chopped salad burnet
Juice of 1 lemon and 1 lime
Salt and freshly ground black pepper to taste

Tear the hearts of the lettuce into medium-size pieces. Add the salad burnet. Toss with the lemon and lime juices and salt and pepper. (Note: This recipe omits oil but you can add it if you think it needs it.) Serves 4.

WILTED LETTUCE SALAD

1 quart crisphead lettuce leaves, torn into large pieces
4 strips bacon, diced
2 teaspoons sugar
½ teaspoon salt
Dash of freshly ground black pepper
¼ teaspoon dry mustard
3 tablespoons red wine vinegar

Put the lettuce leaves into a large bowl. Cook the bacon pieces until crisp and add the remaining ingredients to the bacon fat and heat, stirring, to dissolve the sugar. Pour the mixture over the lettuce and toss well. Serves 4 to 6. (Note: You can substitute other greens for the lettuce. Dandelion, spinach, and kale are particularly good.)

ROCKET SALAD

Toss rocket leaves with lemon juice and a little salt in a chilled salad bowl and serve immediately. Variation: Combine rocket leaves with thinly sliced cucumbers, tomatoes, and minced garlic and toss with salad oil and a little salt.

RUBY LETTUCE SALAD

1 clove garlic, cut in half
2 large heads ruby lettuce (about 8 cups leaves) torn apart
½ cup beets, thinly sliced and cut into strips
1 tablespoon chopped chives
2 teaspoons chopped fresh parsley
2 teaspoons chopped chervil
½ teaspoon chopped thyme
2 tomatoes, peeled and quartered
1 cup beet greens, torn in pieces

Rub a salad bowl with cut garlic. Add the remaining ingredients and toss with Basic French Dressing to which has been added 1 teaspoon sugar and 1 tablespoon beet juice (optional). Serves 4 to 6.

Radichetta Salad

1 large bunch or 2 cups young radichetta leaves and stalks
1/2 pound fresh mushrooms, thinly sliced
2 teaspoons lemon juice
1/4 cup scallion greens, thinly sliced
3 tablespoons olive oil
1/3 teaspoon salt

Chop the leaves and thinly slice stalks of radichetta. In the salad bowl toss the mushrooms with the lemon juice until they are slightly moistened. Add the radichetta leaves and stalks and the scallion greens, oil, and salt. Toss lightly. Chill the salad before serving. Serves 4.

Sorrel Salad with Hard-Cooked Eggs

1 large bunch sorrel leaves and stems
4 hard-cooked eggs, coarsely chopped

Combine the sorrel leaves and stems with the hard-cooked eggs and toss with Basic French Dressing. Serves 4.

Sorrel and Lettuce Salad

4 sorrel leaves
1 head romaine lettuce
1 head crisphead lettuce
2 stalks fennel
2 tablespoons chopped chives
1 tablespoon chopped parsley
1 tablespoon chopped fresh tarragon

Chop the sorrel into small pieces. Tear the lettuce into small pieces. Cut the tops off the fennel and cut the stalks into strips 3 inches long and 1/4 inch thick. Put the sorrel, lettuces, and fennel into a salad bowl and toss with Basic French Dressing. Garnish with the chives, parsley, and tarragon. Serves 6.

SPINACH SALAD

1 pound raw, crisp spinach or spinach substitutes
1 clove garlic, minced
1 onion, grated
2 tablespoons lemon juice
7 tablespoons oil
Tomato wedges
3 hard-cooked eggs, quartered

Cut off the tough stems of the spinach and discard. Blend the next four ingredients. Garnish with the tomato wedges and hard-cooked eggs. Serves 4 to 6.

SPINACH SALAD WITH DILL

1 pound raw, crisp spinach or spinach substitutes
1 tablespoon chopped dill
2 tablespoons oil
1 tablespoon vinegar
Salt and freshly ground black pepper to taste

Cut off the tough stems of the spinach and discard. Add the dill, oil, vinegar, salt, and pepper, and toss lightly. Serves 4 to 6.

SPINACH SALAD WITH FRUIT

1 pound raw, crisp spinach or spinach substitutes
1 small can mandarin oranges, drained
1 small can white grapefruit, drained
1 avocado, sliced
2 heads Belgian endive, sliced

Add the mandarin oranges and grapefruit to the spinach. Chill. Just before serving add the avocado and the Belgian endive. Toss with Basic French Dressing to which has been added ¼ cup crumbled blue cheese (or more, according to taste). Serves 4 to 6.

Spinach and Mushroom Salad

Toss spinach and thinly sliced raw mushrooms with Bacon Dressing.

Spinach Salad with Sprouts

4 to 6 cups raw, crisp spinach or spinach substitutes
3 cups fresh bean sprouts
½ cup salad oil
¼ cup cider vinegar
3 tablespoons chili sauce
½ teaspoon salt (or to taste)
Freshly ground black pepper
2 hard-cooked eggs, quartered

Tear the spinach leaves into medium-size pieces; add to the sprouts. Mix the oil, vinegar, chili sauce, salt, and pepper. Toss with the spinach and sprouts. Garnish with the egg quarters. Serves 4 to 6.

SPROUTS AND LETTUCE SALAD

1 head crisphead lettuce
2 cups alfalfa sprouts
1 tomato, cut into small pieces
1 red onion, thinly sliced

Break up the lettuce into a salad bowl. Add the remaining ingredients and toss with Basic French Dressing. Serves 4. (Note: Other sliced raw vegetables, such as cucumber, celery, green pepper, and cauliflower, are good added to this salad. It is also good topped with a sharp, grated cheese and tossed with a little oil and vinegar or lemon juice, salt, and freshly ground black pepper.)

UPLAND CRESS SALAD

1 bunch (or about 2 cups) upland cress
1 head Buttercrunch lettuce, torn into large pieces
1 cup spinach leaves
1 avocado
Several peppergrass leaves
½ cup Basic French Dressing made with lemon juice in place of vinegar

Toss all the ingredients together and serve immediately. Serves 4.

STUFFED LETTUCE

1 3-ounce package cream cheese, softened
2 tablespoons Roquefort or blue cheese
2 tablespoons chopped raw carrot
1 tablespoon chopped green pepper
2 tablespoons chopped raw tomato
1 tablespoon onion juice
Salt and freshly ground black pepper to taste
Dash of Tabasco
1 head crisphead lettuce, Iceberg variety

Blend the cheeses. Mix in the next six ingredients. Hollow out the head of lettuce leaving a 1-inch "wall" and stuff it with the mixture. Wrap in wax paper and chill. Slice in desired thickness.

FLOWER SALADS

NASTURTIUM SALAD
2 cucumbers
12 nasturtium flowers and 12 young leaves
¼ cup Basic French Dressing
Thinly slice the cucumbers, top with the nasturtium flowers and leaves, and toss lightly with the Basic French Dressing. Serves 4.

NASTURTIUM SALAD WITH LETTUCE
1 head crisphead lettuce, torn into small pieces
½ head curly endive, torn into small pieces
1 head Bibb lettuce, torn into small pieces
Approximately 2 dozen nasturtium leaves
1 cup raw fresh peas
1 small Bermuda onion, thinly sliced
½ cup Basic French Dressing
Put the lettuce, nasturtium leaves, and the peas into a salad bowl. Top with the Bermuda onion. Toss lightly with the Basic French Dressing. Serves 6 to 8.

VIOLET SALAD

Here are two ways to make violet salads:

1. Toss violet flowers and young leaves with a little lemon juice and a pinch of salt.

2. Toss violet flowers with watercress and a very small amount of Basic French Dressing.

And don't forget to use nasturtium, calendula, violet, and rocket flowers as garnishes for your tossed green salads.

GRAND FINALE — TWENTY-FIVE-INGREDIENT SALAD

An expert gardener, who spends his summers on Monhegan Island, Maine, picked the following vegetables and flowers from his garden in August last year to make a salad for a dinner party. I was not among the guests, but I was told by one of them that she has never tasted such a salad. The variety of tastes combined with the freshness of the ingredients was "too delectable to describe."

Here, with many thanks to the master salad maker, are the twenty-five ingredients:

Nasturtium flowers
Nasturtium leaves
Chrysanthemum leaves
Day-lily Buds
Wild rose petals
Mustard blossoms
Borage blossoms
Sorrel
Tarragon
Rocket
Pac Choi (Chinese mustard)
Prizehead lettuce
Salad Bowl lettuce
Slobolt lettuce
Ruby lettuce
Upland cress
Peppergrass (cress)
Garlic greens
Scallions
Chervil
Italian parsley
Swiss chard
Spinach
Malabar spinach
Orach (a spinachlike green that grows wild)

For an adventure in making a savory soup, take a basket or large pot and tour your vegetable garden and your backyard, and pick as many edible greens as you can find. Don't pass by the herbs, and if it's spring, pick a few dandelion and violet leaves. Wash your greens, drain them, and chop them. Then put them in a pot of well-seasoned, boiling chicken stock. Cook briefly and enjoy a soup whose ingredients you can vary as many times as you feel like taking a backyard tour.

Here are some other soups from salad greens:

ROMAINE SOUP

1 tablespoon butter
½ onion, minced
2 cups chicken broth, canned or fresh
4 cups romaine lettuce, chopped
2 egg yolks
½ cup heavy cream

Melt the butter in a saucepan. Add the onion and cook until it is clear but not brown. Add the chicken broth and bring it to a boil. Add the romaine and simmer until it wilts. Beat the egg yolks and heavy cream together and stir into the broth. Cook over low heat, stirring constantly until the soup thickens. Do not let the soup boil. Serves 4 to 6.

SUMMER SOUP

Place in a blender:

2 leaves crisphead lettuce
1 cucumber, peeled, partially seeded, and cut into 2-inch pieces
2 whole scallions
1 cup each sour cream and chicken broth
4 sprigs watercress or upland cress
½ avocado, peeled and seeded
Salt and freshly ground black pepper to taste

Blend at high speed for 2 minutes. Serve chilled, topped with chopped chives. For variety, add a teaspoon of curry powder. Serves 4.

LETTUCE SOUP

4 cups chicken broth, canned or fresh
1 head crisphead lettuce, cut into narrow strips with core removed
2 tablespoons finely chopped chives
Salt and freshly ground black pepper to taste
1 cup light cream (or plain yogurt if you are dieting)
1 tablespoon fresh chervil or parsley, chopped

Boil the chicken broth in a saucepan and add the lettuce strips. Cover the pan and cook 5 to 10 minutes over low heat. Remove from the heat, add the chives, salt and pepper to taste. Allow to cool at room temperature for 10 minutes, then blend in the cream or yogurt. Refrigerate the soup, covered, 2 to 3 hours. To serve, garnish with the chopped chervil or parsley. Serves 4 to 6.

SCHAV (SOUR GRASS OR SORREL SOUP)

2 quarts salted water
2 pounds sour grass or sorrel
Sour salt

2 hard-cooked eggs, sliced (for thickened schav)
Sour cream
Scallions

Boil the sour grass in the salted water for 6 to 8 minutes. Add the sour salt. You now have 2 quarts of basic schav. You can chill it and use it as is with hard-cooked egg slices and sour cream and scallions. To thicken it, beat into the warm (not hot) schav 2 raw eggs and a little sour cream, and then chill it. Serves 8.

This recipe was given to me by a friend who told me it has been handed down through several generations in her family. The measurements are very flexible and can be adjusted to suit the individual cook's taste.

LEFTOVER SALAD GAZPACHO

Put your leftover salad, right from the table with dressing on it, into a blender, add enough tomato juice to make a liquid, and blend at high speed for a minute. Chill and top with bread crumbs, diced cucumber, chopped onions, and chopped green pepper. You can add a clove of garlic in the blender or sprinkle on garlic salt later, unless your dressing is already garlicky.

CREAM OF CELERY SOUP

5 stalks of celery, chopped
1 onion
4 cups milk (or 2 cups milk plus 2 cups chicken broth, fresh or canned)
2½ tablespoons butter
2½ tablespoons potato starch
1 cup cream
Salt and freshly ground black pepper to taste

Simmer the celery and onion in 2 cups of the milk (or chicken broth) for 20 minutes. In another pan, melt the butter. Blend in the potato starch until smooth and add the remaining 2 cups milk. Simmer until smooth, stirring constantly. Add the celery-milk (or celery-broth) mixture and the cream. Add the salt and pepper. Heat to, but not past, the boiling point. Serves 4.

GREENS FOR THE COOKING

You can cook many of the greens you have grown in your backyard garden — lettuce, spinach, spinach substitutes, kale, Chinese cabbage, mustard greens, corn salad, endive-escarole, etc. Remember, they are best when young and tender. To cook your greens, first wash them well and drain them in a colander. Put the greens into a kettle or large saucepan, add no water, cover tightly, and cook from 3 to 10 minutes. To serve, melt some butter to which you can add herbs, lemon juice, Madeira wine, or hot Bacon Dressing, and pour over the greens. Season to taste and serve piping hot.

Note: If your greens are not young, add a cup or so of lightly salted water with a little bacon, salt pork, or butter, and cook until they are tender.

CELTUCE AU GRATIN
8 to 10 stalks celtuce (or 2 cups), peeled and cut into 1-inch pieces
2 cups light cream sauce seasoned with salt and freshly ground black pepper
1 cup grated Swiss cheese
¾ cup bread crumbs
Cook the celtuce in a small amount of boiling salted water until it is just tender. Place in a baking dish and cover with the cream sauce. Combine the cheese and bread crumbs and sprinkle them on top. Brown under the broiler. Serves 4.

Celtuce is also good when boiled or steamed like fresh asparagus and served plain, with lemon, or with herb butter. For a refreshing change of taste, try substituting celtuce for celery in recipes for both raw and cooked celery.

ORIENTAL LETTUCE

4 heads looseleaf lettuce, torn into large pieces
6 tablespoons peanut or soy oil
1 clove garlic, mashed
2 teaspoons soy sauce
¼ cup beef broth

Wash and dry the lettuce pieces. Heat the oil in a frying pan over high heat and cook the garlic until brown. Add the lettuce leaves and sprinkle with soy sauce and broth. Cook quickly, stirring, no longer than 1 minute. Serves 4.

BRAISED BELGIAN ENDIVE

4 heads Belgian endive, halved lengthwise
¼ cup butter
1 cup chicken broth, fresh or canned
Juice of ½ lemon
½ teaspoon sugar
½ teaspoon salt
½ teaspoon freshly ground black pepper

In a heavy skillet, heat the butter and brown the endive halves in it. Combine the remaining ingredients and pour over the endive. Continue cooking, uncovered, until the endive is tender — about 20 minutes. Add more chicken broth if necessary. Garnish with chopped parsley or basil. Serves 2.

BRAISED FENNEL

2 heads fennel, cut into quarters lengthwise
6 tablespoons butter
Salt and freshly ground black pepper to taste

In a large frying pan, heat the butter and add the fennel, turning it until it is browned on all sides. Add the salt and pepper, cover the pan, and continue cooking until the fennel is tender. Serve the fennel with the juices from the pan poured over it. Serves 4.

KALE

Cook kale as you cook spinach, only cook it a little longer. Follow the recipe for Italian Spinach or simply serve it with melted butter and grated nutmeg.

PAN-BRAISED LETTUCE

Heads of butterhead or romaine lettuce (one for each person)
Chicken or beef broth, fresh or canned
Butter
Salt and freshly ground black pepper

Cut the heads of lettuce in half and place in a large skillet. Barely cover with broth, cover the pot, and bring to a boil. Immediately reduce heat to a simmer. Cook the lettuce until it is barely tender (about 2 minutes). Drain the broth from the skillet and save it for soups and sauces. To braise the lettuce, add 1 tablespoon of butter for each head, salt, and pepper. Heat for 5 minutes, turn the lettuce over, and heat for 3 to 4 minutes more. (Note: For variation, use half broth and half white wine.)

BATTERFRY PARSLEY

When you are deep-frying chicken or shrimp, dip sprigs of parsley into the batter and deep-fry them for a delectable accompaniment to your main dish.

PARSLEY CHICKEN

If you have grown so much parsley in your garden that you can't even give it away, here's an excellent recipe for it.

¼ pound butter
2½-pound frying chicken, cut up
6 cloves garlic, chopped
Large bunch (fistful) parsley, chopped
Salt and freshly ground black pepper to taste

Preheat oven to 325°.

In a large skillet melt the butter and fry the chicken very slowly until pale brown. The chicken does not have to be done. Remove the chicken to a baking

dish or casserole. If the butter has turned brown, discard it and melt another ¼
pound. Add the garlic and parsley to the butter and cook until the garlic is soft
and the parsley is limp. Do not overcook — the parsley and garlic should be
fresh-looking. Pour the garlic and parsley mixture over the chicken, add salt
and pepper, cover, and bake for 30 minutes. Serves 4.

PASTA AND GREENS

Raw chopped greens do wonders for pasta. Cook chopped garlic in hot oil,
pour over spaghetti or noodles, and add chopped greens — spinach, dandelion,
chicory, escarole, parsley, etc. Toss together. Add a layer of cooked spinach
when you are making lasagne; add chopped spinach to ravioli.

PURSLANE

Steam the fresh leaves and tender stems of purslane briefly, and serve with
melted garlic butter or lemon juice and chopped parsley.

SPINACH IN A MOLD

1 pound raw spinach, chopped
1 cup chopped celery
½ cup chopped white onion
½ cup chopped parsley
1 tablespoon chopped fresh tarragon
Salt and freshly ground black pepper to taste
1 teaspoon lemon juice
1 cup sour cream

Cook the chopped spinach, let it cool, and squeeze all the water out of it.
Mix the raw ingredients with the spinach. Add the salt, pepper, lemon juice,
and sour cream and mix. Put into a mold and chill well. Serve with Chiffonade
or Tangy Dressing. Serves 4.

Italian Spinach

2 pounds spinach
½ cup consommé
1 clove garlic
1 tablespoon oil or butter

Wash the spinach thoroughly and drain well. Bring the consommé to a boil in a large saucepan. Add the garlic and spinach. Cook about 5 minutes. Remove the garlic, drain the spinach thoroughly, and chop fine. Melt the butter in the saucepan and when it is sizzling hot but not brown, return the spinach to the pan and stir well until heated. Serves 4.

Seed Catalogs

Burgess Seed and Plant Company, P.O. Box 3000, Galesburg, Michigan, 49053. Seeds for sprouting and sprouters to sprout them in.

W. Atlee Burpee Company, 300 Park Avenue, Warminster, Pennsylvania, 18991; Clinton, Iowa, 52732; P.O. Box 748, 6350 Rutland Avenue, Riverside, California, 92505. Large selection of lettuces and other salad greens, many of which are Burpee's exclusives. Contains many garden supplies and helpful hints for the home gardener.

Comstock, Ferre and Company, 263 Main Street, Wethersfield, Connecticut, 06109. Good selection of herbs.

De Giorgi Company, Inc., Council Bluffs, Iowa, 51501. Prize-winning seeds. Excellent selection of lettuces and other salad greens. Gardening advice.

Farmer Seed and Nursery Company, Fairbault, Minnesota, 55021. Good selection of salad vegetables. Gardening supplies, fish emulsion and seaweed fertilizers.

Henry Field Seed and Nursery Company, Shenandoah, Iowa, 51602. Gardening supplies and advice, plans for gardens including a raised "salad bar."

The French Garden Company, Chicken Hill, Nantucket, Massachusetts, 02554. French lettuces and other salad green seeds packaged in attractive burlap sacks. Directions for growing and recipes included.

Gurney Seed and Nursery Company, 1448 Page Street, Yankton, South

Dakota, 57078. Big, colorful catalog with a good selection of salad greens. Gardening supplies and advice.

Joseph Harris Company, Inc., Moreton Farm, Rochester, New York, 14624. Good selection of lettuces and other salad greens, herbs.

Johnny's Selected Seeds, Albion, Maine, 04910. English lettuces, assorted greens from the Far East, herbs. Gives suggestions and invites gardeners to share ideas toward weed control through "natural agriculture."

Nichols Garden Nursery, 1190 North Pacific Highway, Albany, Oregon, 97321. An off-the-beaten-track catalog of herbs and rare seeds. Includes lettuces and greens from the Far East. Sells herb plants as well as seeds. Gardening and kitchen aids and many recipes. Carries liquid seaweed.

George W. Park Seed Company, Inc., Greenwood, South Carolina, 29646. Herbs, gardening aids.

Seedway, Inc., Hall, New York, 14463. Standard selection of lettuces and other greens. Garden supplies.

R. H. Shumway, 628 Cedar Street, Rockford, Illinois, 61101. Large catalog with old-fashioned illustrations. Standard selection of lettuces and other greens.

Stokes Seeds, P.O. Box 548, Main Post Office, Buffalo, New York, 14240. This serious, thorough catalog has seeds for both commercial and home growers with varieties mainly for northern gardeners. Carries lettuce seeds for greenhouse growing plus many disease-resistant varieties. Organic gardeners' page. Sells liquid seaweed.

Thompson and Morgan, P.O. Box 24, 401 Kennedy Boulevard, Somerdale, New Jersey, 08083. Well-organized and complete catalog. Excellent selection of lettuce and other greens with varieties recommended for southern states. Growing instructions, reference, and source information. Directions and supplies for sprouting seeds. Herb seeds. A "germination brochure" is sent with each order.

Natural Pest Controls

Note: If address is not given, it appears under Seed Catalogs in previous section.

LADYBUGS AND PRAYING MANTISES

Bio-Control Company, Route 2, Box 2397, Auburn, California, 95603
W. Atlee Burpee Company
Eastern Biological Control Company, Route 5, Box 379, Jackson, New Jersey, 08527
Gothard, Inc., P.O. Box 370, Canutillo, Texas, 79835
Gurney Seed and Nursery Company

TO MAKE WHITEFLY TRAPS:

"Tack Trap," **Animal Repellent, Inc.,** Griffin, Georgia, 30223
"Tree Tanglefoot," **Henry Field Seed and Nursery Company, R. H. Shumway**

"Handbook of Herbs" that repel bugs, **Merry Gardens,** Camden, Maine, 04843 (One dollar)

Fairfax Biological Laboratory, Clinton Corners, New York, 12514
Gothard, Inc. (see above)

BIOLOGICAL CONTROL SPRAY — *BACILLUS THURINGIENSIS* (DIPEL, BIOTROL, THURICIDE)

Farmer Seed and Nursery Company
Nichols Garden Nursery

"HAVAHART" ANIMAL TRAPS

W. Atlee Burpee Company
Farmer Seed and Nursery Company
Henry Field Seed and Nursery Company

Frost Map

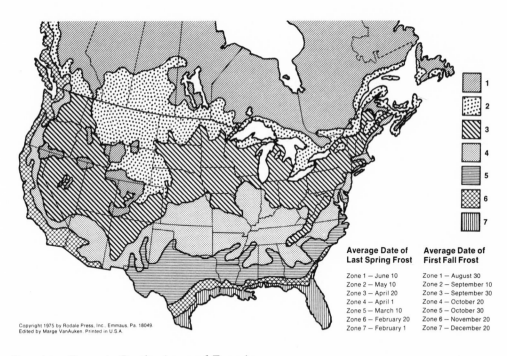

	1
	2
	3
	4
	5
	6
	7

Average Date of Last Spring Frost	**Average Date of First Fall Frost**
Zone 1 — June 10	Zone 1 — August 30
Zone 2 — May 10	Zone 2 — September 10
Zone 3 — April 20	Zone 3 — September 30
Zone 4 — April 1	Zone 4 — October 20
Zone 5 — March 10	Zone 5 — October 30
Zone 6 — February 20	Zone 6 — November 20
Zone 7 — February 1	Zone 7 — December 20

Copyright 1975 by Rodale Press, Inc., Emmaus, Pa. 18049.
Edited by Marge VanAuken. Printed in U.S.A.

Courtesy Organic Gardening and Farming

General Index

Index to Recipes